THY KINGDOM COME

THY KINGDOM COME

LIFE AND FINANCIAL GUIDE TO THE KINGDOM OF GOD

*A*dvantage
BOOKS

PATRICK MCFALL

Thy Kingdom Come by Patrick McFall
Copyright © 2020 by Patrick McFall
All Rights Reserved.
ISBN: 978-1-59755-586-9

Published by: ADVANTAGE BOOKS™
                   Longwood, Florida, USA
                   www.advbookstore.com

Library of Congress Catalog Number: 2020941284

First Printing: December 2020
20 21 22 23 24 25   10 9 8 7 6 5 4 3 2 1
Printed in the United States of America

Table of Contents

SECTION 2: KINGDOM LIFE

SECTION 4: CONCLUSION

Endorsements

"After being married to, and hence a recipient of this revelatory gift for almost 25 years, I am ecstatic that transformation awaits everyone who would dare to delve into this awakening truth of the Kingdom message. I applaud Patrick's passion and dogmatic approach to what every believer should know and live. His ability to reach beyond the depths of man's religion into a sphere that brings each reader face to face with the greatness and goodness of The Almighty God is immeasurable."

– Rev. Lavette McFall (Mrs.),
Masters in Christian Studies (Honours),
Luthor Rice College and Seminary

"*Thy Kingdom Come* is certainly a Spirit led, deep dive into the Scriptures."

– Kenneth Strachan,
MBA, University of Miami

"*Thy Kingdom Come* has radically changed my life. This book captures, in a profound way, how to live and apply Kingdom principles to our everyday living. I highly recommend this book to all who want to live following the commandments of Jesus. You will never be the same!"

– Jacqueline Fraser
Master of Theology,
North Carolina Theological Seminary,

"Thanks Rev. McFall. Your teaching presented a new understanding of the New Covenant of Jesus' teachings, compared to the old teachings of the law."

– Howard Miller,
Trustee, Bethel Baptist Church

"*Thy Kingdom Come* positively shows me how understanding who we are as God's children, and therefore how our responsibilities, gifts and purpose, all affect our approach to finances, and just life period!"

– Gillian Moss (Mrs.),
MBA, Nova Southeastern University

"Congratulations to Patrick for his deep thought, contemplation and financial mind; a heart filled with the determination to know and understand how to live in and manifest the Kingdom of God and its financial structure, then make it known to All."

– **Maria Butler**
Operations Manager,
Trinity Christian School

Acknowledgements

A world of thanks goes to my beloved wife, Rev. Lavette Elise McFall, an acclaimed preacher, teacher, prophet and scholar in God's Kingdom. Her contributions to this book, by way of her support, advice, and input, is sprinkled in every concept, strewn on every page and sprayed in every allusion. She has encouraged me from day one, being ever confident that this book will be a fulfilment of God's purpose for my life and a blessing for the body of Christ. I am forever grateful to you for your love and support.

I give special honour to my Pastor, Rev. Dr. Timothy Stewart, for his leadership and support. I say it often that you are my leader both by choice and by God's divine purpose. Thank you for allowing me time and space to pursue this book, and for releasing me to teach it to others. Your support and pastoral covering make all the difference in the world.

Special mention is made to the following persons who were my sounding board for the difficult and sensitive topics that are covered in this book. I enjoyed the times when we deliberated, searched the scriptures, called on our experiences, and collectively grasped God's revelation concerning these matters. You are all so very gifted and supportive. Thank you so much.

Lady Sharon Stewart
Pastor Jacqueline Fraser
Sister Beverly Francis
Deaconess Valderene Gardiner

Special acknowledgement goes to those members of my first Kingdom Empowerment for Everyday Living class. I have been so blessed to share God's revelations with you and to simultaneously learn from you. Your feedback and questions have challenged me to build a better mousetrap. This book would not be as thorough nor as meaningful without you.

To the greatest church on this side of heaven, Bethel Baptist Church, Nassau Bahamas, thank you for accepting me and allowing me to serve you.

Last, but not least, to my mother, Yvonne McFall, thank you for everything.

Patrick James McFall

Foreword

My relationship with Rev. Patrick dates more than three decades. He has always stood out as a gifted and progressive individual. I have observed his stellar academic achievements, his love for God and family, and his sacrificial commitment to others. I was really delighted when the Lord revealed to me that Patrick, while at the pinnacle of his professional banking career, would eventually work closely with me in ministry. That close collaboration started in 2015, and ever since, Patrick and his wife Lavette have been invaluable to my life, family and ministry.

What I love most about Patrick is his confident humility and conscious unselfishness. He has decided to forsake a propitious career in banking, where he was already achieving immense personal fulfilment, to serve God as a lay minister and volunteer.

I am extremely excited about this book and what it signifies to the church. I recommend it highly because it speaks to what the world needs most. We need more people dedicated to the pure doctrine of Jesus Christ, one of love, humility and service to God and man. This message is timely and exactly what the church needs to prepare us for our Lord's return, something that every Christian should be focused on, given the calamities we are experiencing in the world today.

Thy Kingdom Come is a reservoir of spiritual treasures.

Rev. Dr. Timothy Stewart
Pastor, Bethel Baptist Church,
President, Progressive National Baptist Convention

Patrick James McFall

Introduction

"Repent: for the Kingdom of heaven is at hand!"

The Bible tells us in Matthew 4:17 that these are what Jesus preached regularly and consistently–repentance, the Kingdom of Heaven, and the fact that the Kingdom was soon to come.

The Kingdom is a really big deal! It was prophesied in the books of Daniel, Isaiah, Ezekiel, Psalm, Ecclesiastes, and Jeremiah, at a minimum. According to Daniel, when the Kingdom of God comes, it will destroy all kingdoms of this world forever; and it will be the only Kingdom that remains (Daniel 2:44). The Kingdom was also prophesied in the new testament, and we don't use the word prophesied lightly. Jesus, Paul, John, James, and Peter all prophesied about the coming Kingdom of God. It is directly referenced 88 times in the four Gospels, and about 70 times in the Epistles. The Apostles talked about being heirs and having an inheritance in the Kingdom, indicating that its arrival is pending.

Everything in the new testament is about the Kingdom of God. That's no exaggeration! In Matthew 6:33, Jesus said that we must seek the Kingdom first, and all **these things** will be added to us. The things He was referring to were food, home, and clothing (Matthew 6:25-32). The Kingdom is so important that it supersedes all of these basic and critical needs of our lives. This is what makes this topic so fascinating, that something can be more important than the things we need to survive. How is that even possible?

Thy Kingdom Come ("This Book") explains and explores this dynamic. My aim in writing This Book is to establish the importance of the Kingdom and its historical and personal significance to our lives. Its primary purpose is to help Christians refocus on the true message of God's Kingdom and to prepare us for its arrival. This Book also addresses some of the teachings that are inconsistent with Jesus' doctrines about the Kingdom. This is important because our enemy, the Devil, has been busy trying to deceive us about the truth concerning this most important topic.

This Book uncovers many hidden mysteries about the Kingdom of Heaven and tackles some very tough questions relating to it. While some of these questions are academic, most are practical and instructional, to help us live the Kingdom life that Jesus championed. It's the life the early Christians lived.

Below are some of the intriguing issues addressed in This Book:

- Jesus told us to keep <u>His</u> commandments (John 14:15). We know what Moses' commandments were—but what are His?

- Jesus said He did not come to destroy the law or the prophets. However, six times in Matthew 5 (see verses 21-48), we see Him disagreeing with some of the laws. How do we reconcile these apparent inconsistencies?

- God promised to make Abraham a great nation. The Apostles seemed to narrowly connect this prophesy about the Kingdom to Israel (Acts 1:6). Were they mistaken?

- Jesus preached that the Kingdom of Heaven is at hand. This, combined with the miracles that He performed, drove His followers to attempt to forcibly anoint Him as their King (see John 6:15). He refused. Adding insult to injury, He left earth and ascended into Heaven without taking a throne. What does His departure mean in relation to the coming of the Kingdom?

- Today, some people believe that the Kingdom has already come and that it coexists as part of our world, much the same way spirit and body coexists. Has it really come, or are we misinterpreting the scriptures in hopes of taking over the world, just like the disciples once did?

- If the Kingdom is here, where is it? If it isn't here, when is it coming?

- Is the Kingdom synonymous with the church?

This Book brings these and more thought-provoking facts about the Kingdom of God into focus. It kicks off with a background discovery of the Kingdom, putting into perspective its correlation with Abraham, Moses, and the Laws. After establishing its history, This Book delves into Kingdom life. It documents the only way one may enlist in the Kingdom, and how, once a member, one must live as a Kingdom citizen.

Jesus regularly told His disciples that if they loved Him, they must keep His commandments. We, too, must keep them if we love Him. But **few people can even articulate what Jesus' commandments are**. Nowhere are His commandments listed in the new testament the way the Ten Commandments are in the old testament. Yet, they are everywhere. This may be why we don't, on average, adhere to the same high standards as our new testament counterparts. This Book, however, seeks to rectify this. It lays out His commandments and presents them to readers in an easy to follow format. We reveal His commandments to ensure that God's people know exactly what they are and understand what is expected of us. In that respect, This Book ushers us back into the days of the early church in terms of its doctrines and emphasis.

Jesus left us, but He didn't leave us alone. We see in these pages the essential work of the Holy Spirit. We dive into the gifts of the Spirit, showing how vital they are to the "perfecting of the saints, for the work of the ministry, for the edifying of the body of Christ" (Ephesians 4:12). **We all have an interconnected purpose in life.** We need each other! Our collective purpose is intertwined by the gifts the Holy Spirit gave us. We cannot be complete without each other, no matter how independent we believe ourselves to be. **We become perfected when we use our spiritual gifts to help others**. The gifts are like essential minerals to the body. When some are lacking, everyone suffers. Therefore, everyone MUST pursue their gifts, or else we all will suffer.

But to only view the Holy Spirit through the lens of His gifts is a narrow perspective of Him. Jesus thought it advantageous that He leaves so that the Holy Spirit may come (John 16:7). He is here to establish our connection to God. We cannot be children of God without the Holy Spirit, nor can we enter God's Kingdom without Him (John 3:5).

Because Jesus spoke so commonly about money as part of His Kingdom message (more than 50% of the time), we could no less complete a book about the Kingdom without examining finances from a Kingdom perspective. This is a popular topic in Christendom today, and it is readily understandable why. **Money is as important to God as it is to us, but in very different ways.** When most of us think about money and finances, we think about how to earn it, manage it, grow it, and save it. We also consider how to spend it, sometimes even before we earn it. All of these goals about money are the product of the teachings of the world. In short, worldly financial management teaches us how to GET and SAVE.

This Book, on the other hand, teaches Kingdom finances as taught by Christ, and there are some very surprising differences between what Jesus taught about money and finances from those taught by the world. **Kingdom finances teach us to GIVE, without expecting a reward or return**. Unfortunately, most of us only want to learn how to get, and therefore we search really hard for scriptures that support this, meanwhile ignoring the words of Christ. **Jesus never taught us how to make money. In fact, He taught the exact opposite**; He said we must give it away.

God expects us to give to help others (Matthew 5:42). That includes money! He even wants us to give to our enemies (Luke 6:35). Failure to properly manage our personal finances prevents us from maximizing our economic resources. This, in turn, negatively affects our ability to adhere to the Kingdom principles about giving. Consequently, we have included a practical guide in This Book about managing personal finances, from a Kingdom perspective. The financial chapters in This Book were written for financial novices, people with some financial responsibilities, but little to no education or training in finances.

Before reading another self-help book that tells us how to conquer the world for Christ, read **Thy Kingdom Come**. It will enlighten you as to why Jesus said that the greatest in His Kingdom is the one who is least. This Book helps us live the way Jesus envisioned. Only by doing so can we become "great" in God's Kingdom.

Section 1

Kingdom Fundamentals

In Daniel chapter 2, Nebuchadnezzar II saw a vision of a figure with a golden head, chest and arms of silver, belly and thighs of brass, legs of iron, and feet of part iron and part clay. God gave the king this vision to foretell the rise and fall of different kingdoms, starting with Babylon (Nebuchadnezzar's kingdom). In the end, however, God would establish His kingdom, which will destroy all other kingdoms. His kingdom will last forever!

Daniel 2:44 (CEB) But in the days of those kings, the God of heaven will raise up an everlasting kingdom that will be indestructible. Its rule will never pass to another people. It will shatter other kingdoms. It will put an end to all of them. It will stand firm forever

At its most basic level, a Kingdom is about an organized group of people, headed by a king or queen, who share common interests. It's this simple view which illustrates the relationship between God and His children. On many occasions, Jesus strategically used the concept of Kingdom to define this relationship. Matthew 13 gives a few examples. In the Lord's prayer, Jesus taught us to pray, "Thy Kingdom Come."

God always intended to separate a group of people for Himself. As we look throughout history, there were three major eras, led by three dispensational prophets (one being the Son of God), which show how God went about establishing this objective. They were:

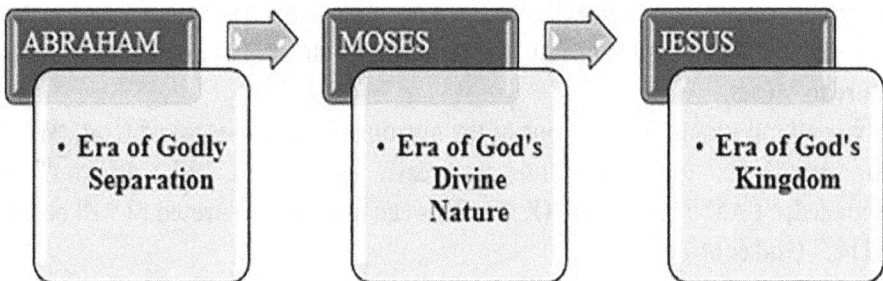

ABRAHAM	MOSES	JESUS
• Era of Godly Separation	• Era of God's Divine Nature	• Era of God's Kingdom

Abraham

God first laid the foundation of a kingdom when He called Abraham. He established a covenant with Abraham that if he would walk with God, meaning if he would accept God's sovereignty, God would, in turn, bless Abraham and his seed.

*Genesis 17:1,2,6,7 (KJV) ¹And when Abram was ninety years old and nine, the Lord appeared to Abram and said unto him, **I am the Almighty God; walk before me, and be thou perfect**. ²And I will make my covenant between me and thee, and will multiply thee exceedingly.*

*⁶And I will make thee exceeding fruitful, and I will make nations of thee, and kings shall come out of thee. ⁷**And I will establish my covenant between me and thee and thy seed after thee in their generations for an everlasting covenant, to be a God unto thee, and to thy seed after thee**.*

Prior to this, there was no group that God specifically identified as His own. Abraham, therefore, ushered in a new era, which I call the **Era of Godly Separation**.

Moses

Although Abraham and his people were separated for God, he only got a partial vision of who God is. In Exodus 6:3, God told Moses:

And I appeared unto Abraham, unto Isaac, and unto Jacob, <u>by the name of God Almighty, but by my name Jehovah was I not known to them.</u>

The literal name Jehovah (YHWH) was used early and often in the Book of Genesis. Therefore, God was not being literal when He said this about His name. Instead, what God was talking about was His nature. The Bible has many examples of individuals whose character was tied to their name. Jesus, for example, means to rescue or deliver. That was the name chosen by God for Him because it reveals Jesus's purpose. Likewise, the name Jehovah has a meaning. This meaning was not revealed to Abraham, Isaac, or Jacob but was revealed to Moses. God revealed His divine nature to Moses.

When God spoke to Moses out of the burning bush, Moses asked God, 'What is your name?' (Exodus 3:13). Moses was really asking God, 'Who are you?' God responded, "I AM THAT AM" (KJV). This can also be interpreted "I will be who I will be." God continued:

Exodus 3:15 (KJV) this is my name for ever, and this is my memorial unto all generations.

In this scripture, God was introducing Moses to the way He wants to be known to the world forever. He didn't explain it to him right away, which is what led Moses to asked Him again to "shew me now thy way, that I may know thee" (Exodus 33:13). God agreed! The revelation of who God is and how He wants to be known forever is found below in Exodus 34:6-7 (KJV):

*⁶And the Lord passed by before him, and proclaimed, **The Lord, The Lord God, merciful and gracious, longsuffering, and abundant in goodness and truth, ⁷Keeping mercy for thousands, forgiving iniquity and transgression and sin, and that will by no means clear the guilty; visiting the iniquity of the fathers upon the children, and upon the children's children, unto the third and to the fourth generation.***

Everything God has done and will do speaks to these characteristics. Moses was the tool used by God to shift the world to the **Era of God's Divine Nature**.

Jesus

Jesus ushered in the next era in the building blocks of God's design for His relationship with mankind. Having already established His desire to set aside a people for Himself, and having established how He would govern His people (by His Nature), God sent Jesus into the world to deliver us from the bondage of sin, which is death (Romans 6:23).

We are reminded of Nebuchadnezzar's dream. All other kingdoms were forever crushed by a rock. The rock signifies the Kingdom of God. Just as the golden head in the vision was Babylon represented by king Nebuchadnezzar, Jesus is the Rock that will crush all kingdoms of this world (1 Corinthians 10:4).

The stage is now set for the final era, the **Era of God's Kingdom**, a time when Jesus will sit on His throne as King over His people. In the words of Jesus:

*Matthew 25:31-34,41 (KJV) ³¹When the Son of man shall come in his glory, and all the holy angels with him, **then shall he sit upon the throne of his glory: ³²And before him shall be gathered all nations: and he shall separate them one from another, as a shepherd divideth his sheep from the goats: ³³And he shall set the sheep on his right hand, but the goats on the left. ³⁴Then shall the King say unto***

them on his right hand, Come, ye blessed of my Father, inherit the kingdom prepared for you from the foundation of the world:

[41] Then shall he say also unto them on the left hand, Depart from me, ye cursed, into everlasting fire, prepared for the devil and his angels:

This final Era began when Jesus came to earth over 2000 years ago. He started it by preparing us for what would eventually be His crowning moment when He takes His throne as our King. To prepare us, Jesus left instructions on how we are to live our lives. Only those who live by the standards He set for His kingdom will enter.

Chapter 1

Kingdom Foundation (Grace & Truth)

John 1:17 (KJV) For the law was given by Moses, but grace and truth came by Jesus Christ.

No holds barred! John went straight for the jugular of the Jewish religious establishment. He went after Moses. In the opening verses of the Gospel of John (v 1-17), the author, being led by the Holy Spirit, made a series of statements that culminated with this earth-shattering comparison between Moses and Jesus.

If John is right that the Law of Moses is to be contrasted to the Grace and Truth of Jesus Christ, given how significant the Laws are to the kingdom/nation of Israel, one would expect Grace and Truth to be incredibly revolutionary to the Kingdom of God. Not only ought we to understand what Jesus gave us in Grace and Truth, but we must also holistically comprehend the circumstances associated with such a great gift. We must pursue this with more fervour than that of the Jewish Scribes and Pharisees with respect to the Law. We must understand what such a gift portends to us and our lives. Are there any strings attached to it? Is it entirely free? Do we need it? Should we accept it? Are we better off without it?

These are some of what we set out to answer in the ensuing pages, and our research has led us to uncover some amazing facts and revelations about the interconnectivity of John's introductory statements in this gospel, to the Kingdom of Heaven that was the cornerstone of Jesus' life, message, and ministry. This, in turn, has widened our understanding of the Kingdom. We have a better appreciation of what it really is and why it is that Jesus constantly preached about it. If something is important to Jesus, it ought to be important to His followers.

Because Jesus is a part of the Godhead, He fully understands what God expects from us. Because Jesus lived as a man, He fully understands our challenges as humans. Jesus remains the only person to be both human and deity. From this unique vantage point, Jesus was able to breakdown the mysteries of God that were hidden in the old testament and revealed them to us in the new testament in a manner that befits our humanity. This is the extraordinary gift that John called Grace and Truth.

By His constant referral to the Kingdom of God, Jesus in effect gave us a roadmap to discovering the gift of Grace and Truth, and how it should impact our lives. Here it is below:

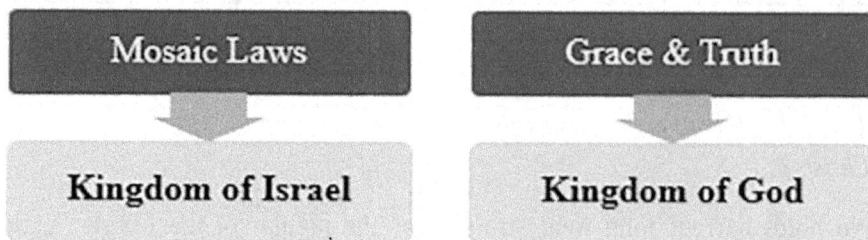

Mosaic Laws	Grace & Truth
Kingdom of Israel	Kingdom of God

The Mosaic Laws ("Laws") were given to the Hebrews as an essential prerequisite to the establishment of the Jewish Kingdom and the inheritance of the promised land. God confirmed the importance of the timing of Moses' gift of the Laws in Joshua, chapter 1, verses 7 & 8. This is what He told Joshua as He prepared him to lead the children of Israel to cross over Jordan River to inherit the promised land:

*Joshua 1:7-8 (KJV) ⁷Only be thou strong and very courageous, that thou mayest observe to do according to all the law, which Moses my servant commanded thee: turn not from it to the right hand or to the left, **that thou mayest prosper withersoever thou goest**. ⁸This book of the law shall not depart out of thy mouth; but thou shalt meditate therein day and night, that thou mayest observe to do according to all that is written therein: <u>for then thou shalt make thy way prosperous, and then thou shalt have good success</u>.*

They were headed to the promised land, and God was telling them that they needed to follow the commandments (or Laws) to be prosperous and successful there.

Not only did Moses give them the Laws before they entered the promised land, but they also had to start living according to the Laws before they inherited it. Many Hebrews left Egypt but died in the wilderness because they did not follow the Laws. Following the Laws was a MUST for inheriting and remaining in the promised land.

Grace and Truth, which is the new testament equivalent to the Laws, precedes us before obtaining a better inheritance. They lead us to and prepare us for the Kingdom of Heaven, which is the eternal promised land. If we want to live in this Kingdom, every Christian, whether Jew or Gentile, must understand them, know how to apply them to our lives, and most importantly, we must not deviate from them, neither to the right hand nor to the left. **We must live according to all of the principles of God's Kingdom, and it must start here on earth**. We must live here the way we must live there; otherwise, we cannot survive or be successful there. Just as the Hebrews lived in the wilderness en route to the promised land for 40 years after their deliverance from Egypt, today, we are pilgrims on earth headed to the promised Kingdom of Heaven. Paul intimated that we all are in search of a better country, which he called heavenly (Hebrews 11:16).

John's Reflexion

John wanted his people to know who Jesus truly was. At that time, Jesus' rightful recognition as the Son of God was disputed by many, or at the least, it was unknown to them. The timing of John's letter (Gospel of John) was in the days of the early church. It had not been long after Jesus was crucified. The Jewish leaders who orchestrated His death had little tolerance for His disciples. Some of those zealots sought out His disciples and meted terrible punishment on them. They wanted to keep them silent about the truth of Jesus. The disciples were mistreated, threatened, stoned, and even killed for continually speaking about and following Jesus. To say that Jesus was not broadly accepted as the Son of God at that time is a colossal understatement.

John understood this and thought it necessary first to establish who Jesus was before dropping this bombshell of a revelation about the gift of Grace and Truth and its superiority to Mosaic Laws. Jesus, John explained, was a member of the Godhead, and He existed from the beginning of time, so much so that He made the world and everything in it. He was in the world, which was made by Him, but the people in the world didn't even know Him. By establishing that Jesus was God, John intimated that the gift that Jesus gave us came directly from God, and could not be ignored, even if it meant that by writing such a book, John's life was mortally endangered.

But John wasn't sure they fully got it. He continued in his letter to explain that the well-known and highly regarded prophet, John the Baptist, whom the Jews respected, believed in Jesus as the Christ. John the Baptist confirmed publicly that Jesus was the Son of God. This, John thought, along with the fact that Jesus rose from the dead and was seen by many other witnesses for 40 days after His resurrection, should be enough to establish the godship of Jesus.

Having established the supremacy of Jesus, John could finally make his point. Moses brought the Mosaic Laws to the Jews and their partisans, but Jesus, the Son of God and creator of the world, brought what James called in the Epistle of James 1:25 the Laws of Liberty (that is, Grace and Truth) to EVERYONE.

The Law

The comments in verse 17 of the first chapter of the gospel of John were directed at making both a comparison and a contrast between Moses and Jesus. Both had significant and special gifts for their generation. Both had gifts that came from God.

The significance of Moses was well-established, even legendary. He was revered in the Jewish community as a true prophet of God. Moses gave the Laws that became the foundation of the Jewish religion and Kingdom. Moses' Laws were crucial to ensure that the Jews understood who they were, whose they were, and what was expected from them. Moses gave the Laws as an instructional guide to keep at the forefront of Israel's minds, that they are to serve Yahweh, and only Him. The book of Deuteronomy outlines many of the laws that Moses delivered in his speech to the Hebrews in preparation for inheriting the promised land (Deuteronomy 6:1). The book includes instructions and laws that would govern their daily living in the land. In Deuteronomy 6, Moses directed the Hebrews to teach the Laws to their children; talk about them at home, while on the road; tie them as symbols on their hands and foreheads; write them on their doorframes and bind them on their foreheads. Having experienced first-hand accounts of the wayward spirit of his people, Moses had major concerns and doubt that the Israelites would continue to upkeep God's commandments, just as their fathers failed so many times in the past.

From the day they left Egypt, the Hebrews complained incessantly about the challenges they faced. They complained about the lack of food. They complained about the lack of water. They constantly compared their lives in the wilderness with their lives back in Egypt. Despite the bondage, slavery, and abuse they were subjected to, they often looked back with nostalgia, because they did not have faith in God to sustain them for the uncertain and challenging journey ahead. They were focused on what they could get as opposed to what they should give. They were supposed to give their loyalty to the God who delivered them from the tyranny of the Egyptians.

Sometimes we, too, as Believers want to hold onto the world. Why? Perhaps the world offers us gratification for our human needs for survival, ambition, and pleasures. However, God is asking us to be separate; to be different by having faith in Him instead of the world's solutions. We too often put our confidence in what we can see, especially with respect to money. We hold on to jobs and salaries as our source and withhold our faith from the One who provides the jobs. We doggedly pursue career success more than the One who gives success freely. We also praise those among us who achieve worldly success, and sadly, we often shun those who do not.

God has not changed. He still expects that when we give our lives to follow Him, that we would forsake the world's ways and keep His standards and commandments. He still expects us to pursue the Kingdom of Heaven more than food, water, clothing, jobs, income, or money (see Matthew 6:33), just as He expected the Hebrews to follow the Laws in the wilderness. Many of us today believe that the Israelites were short-sighted because they regularly cried to Moses about why he took them from Egypt to starve or to die from thirst. We, however, fail to see that when we put our trust in money (mammon), good jobs, savings, retirement assets, politicians, networking, and such, rather than in God, we are operating exactly as they did, with a complete lack of faith and with ungrateful hearts. We are looking at what we can get rather than what we should give.

By the time they were finally ready, the generation of Hebrews that would inherit the promised land was new. Their disobedient fathers were not allowed to inherit the land because they did not give to God what He expected of them. It's the same today. **Disobedience will not inherit the Kingdom of Heaven.** That new generation of Hebrews was symbolic of us changing from our old ways to become new people in Christ, as a prerequisite of inheriting the Kingdom. The old man with our former ways, attitudes, disobedience, selfishness, lusts, and sin in general, **will not** inherit the Kingdom. Our old man must die, or we will. This is a strong warning that echoes the words Apostle Paul wrote in Galatians 5: 19-21.

[19] Now the works of the flesh are manifest, which are these; Adultery, fornication, uncleanness, lasciviousness, [20]Idolatry, witchcraft, hatred, variance, emulations, wrath, strife, seditions, heresies, [21]Envyings, murders, drunkenness, revellings, and such like: of the which I tell you before, as I have also told you in time past, <u>that they which do such things shall not inherit the kingdom of God.</u>

By the time the new generation of Israelites were ready to inherit the promised land, Moses was a bit weary with them. He spent a good portion of Deuteronomy encouraging them to remember to give God their hearts and to follow Him. But eventually, he would escalate this with threats of destruction, doom, and death if they did not. Death eventually became the cornerstone of the Laws.

Galatians 3:10 (KJV) For as many as are of the works of the law are under the curse: for it is written, Cursed is every one that continueth not in all things which are written in the book of the law to do them. (see also Deuteronomy 27:26)

The Laws were about works. Even though they were originally meant to help the Hebrews maintain a strong relationship with God, they instead became rules and rituals...lists of dos and don'ts. The supposed benefit of following the "rituals" was that God would be pleased, but when not followed, punishment (often death) was meted out on all its violators. Because of this, it became almost like a symbol of status or competition as to who followed the Laws and who did not. In Luke 18:9-14, Jesus made this point in the parable about the self-righteous Pharisee. Jesus was not pleased with his behaviour.

Even Moses, the lawgiver, became misled about what is most important to God. God did not allow Moses to lead the Israelites into the promised land because of his behaviour at the desert of Zin (Numbers 20:12). The people were thirsty because they didn't have access to water (verse 2). They complained about it to Moses (verses 3-5). Moses and Aaron became visibly upset with their complaining brothers and sisters, even though God commanded them to supply the people with water (verses 10-11). Bible scholars have different views on the reason God was so upset with them. In my humble view, God was upset because Moses and Aaron failed to honour Him. They did not show the Hebrews key components of God's image as He wanted them to. He wanted them to show how long-suffering, kind, and merciful He is. Instead, Moses and Aaron became judgmental, impatient, and unkind, qualities that God finds repulsive, and they projected that image to the people. They misrepresented who God is, and it cost them big.

I believe God's decision to prevent Moses from entering the land devastated him. Perhaps it clouded his judgment, maybe just a little. Conceivably, it was part of the reason he injected some personal laws that were not given directly by God (for example, see Matthew 19:8). It was important to him that the Israelites who would finally enter into the land understood how fortunate they were. This was the land that God promised Abraham, Isaac, and Jacob. It was the land that Moses would not enter. It was the place where Israel would be established as a nation and eventually as the kingdom of Israel.

Grace and Truth

While Moses gave the Laws, Jesus, on the other hand, brought His own laws, Grace and Truth, the foundation of the salvation of the world, and the underlying principles of the Kingdom of Heaven. The Laws were an integral part of the spiritual progression of mankind. They brought an awakening to what sin is. According to Apostle Paul, "I had not known sin, but by the law: for I had not known lust, except the law had said, Thou shalt not covet." (Romans 7:7b). God, therefore, used the Laws as a stepping stone to Grace and Truth. Galatians 3:24 states, "Wherefore the law was our schoolmaster to bring us unto Christ." From Moses to Christ, we move from the Era of God's Divine Nature to the Era of God's Kingdom.

Like Moses' Laws, we learn from Christ's Laws of Liberty the TRUTH about who we are, whose we are, and what is expected from us. Unlike Moses' Laws, which were established on them doing certain things, Jesus' laws are established on GRACE. Moses' Laws condemned everyone (Romans 4:15). Jesus' Grace and Truth set everyone free from condemnation (Romans 8:1). Jesus removed the fear of curses and death and replaced them with grace and love. Relationships thrive where forgiveness dwells. God wanted us to have a relationship with Him, which is why Jesus gave us Grace and Truth.

Not only is the gift of Grace and Truth better than Moses' Laws, but the promised land also is far better. The children of Israel would inherit the land promised to them by God. This was an earthly land with buildings made with earthly hands. This land could be taken away from them. In fact, it was taken away for centuries and is still highly fought over today. **What Jesus promises is a place in the Kingdom of God, a heavenly place not made with earthly hands** and therefore not subject to the same principles of deterioration, theft, or war.

John 14:1-3 (KJV) Let not your hearts be troubled: ye believe in God, believe also in me. ² In my Father's house are many mansions: if it were not so, I would have told you. <u>I go</u> to prepare a place for you. ³ And if I go and prepare a place for you, I will come again, and receive you unto myself; that where I am, there ye may be also.

Jesus is preparing a place for us, but it's not here. Admission is by invitation only. Those who love Him and keep His commandments will God seal with the Holy Spirit of Promise, an emblem of approval for entry into the Kingdom. As the first begotten Son of God, Jesus came to enlarge God's family through adoption. Anyone who believes in Him could become a child of God, brothers and sisters of Christ. Like Jesus, we would eventually live and be with Him, and our Father God, in eternity. This naturally is far greater than being children of Israel as much as the one who creates exceeds the one created. Being a son of God is what John was selling to his brethren, a major life promotion from being children of Israel. Jesus is still selling this to everyone today.

As sons and daughters, we become heirs of greater promises (gifts) than those made to Abraham, Isaac, and Jacob. In addition to becoming heirs of better promises, we are heirs of the Promise Giver. Although it took 400 years, God kept His promise to give Abram the land, with Moses playing a major role in God's delivery of that promise. Likewise, we wait, but not without hope, knowing that God is able to and will perform exactly what He promised us. The fact that it took the Hebrews so long to inherit their promised land is a subtle yet profound, and often overlooked, message to us, that though He tarries, He will come again and fulfill His promise to give us a better inheritance in Heaven.

The time has now come, John inferred, that God is fulfilling His ultimate promise, this time through Jesus Christ, to make us a great nation in the Kingdom of God. But before we can inherit the Kingdom, we must first prove our worth. The test of the Hebrew's inheritance was their obedience to the Laws of Moses. Our test, indeed our commandment, is conformity to the teachings of Jesus. The fact that God rejected the Hebrews who did not obey the Laws demonstrates His determination to disinvite us from His Kingdom if we do not accede to the Grace and Truth that Jesus brought.

PERSONAL APPLICATION
CHOSEN, BUT NOT PERFECT

Moses was imperfect, but he was chosen and he walked very closely with God. God used him in miraculous ways to deliver His people from the tyranny of the Egyptians. God parted the Red Sea for His people using imperfect Moses. He gave Moses the Ten Commandments, the message of which has transcended time, space, nationalities, and endless naysayers and antagonists. God even allowed Moses to be the first person in history to see His backside and His glory. Despite their closeness and everything that God did through Moses, God did not allow him to lead the Hebrews into the promised land. Moses sinned and paid a hefty price! But make no mistake, Moses remains close with God as confirmed when he appeared with Jesus at His transfiguration.

The children of Israel were chosen by God. They were imperfect, but God nevertheless promised to bless them immensely and to be their God. God delivered many battles and wars for them. He even chose that His son Jesus would come from their lineage. Despite this coveted position as the people of God and being ancestors to the Saviour of the world, the Israelites still are not the superpower of the world like some of them had hoped. Today, they continue to need the association of other nations, like the United States, because of fear that their enemies in the Middle East will attack and severely cripple their existence without the support of their allies. Jesus came to save them, but they overwhelmingly rejected Him. The Jews who rejected Him will have no inheritance in His Kingdom. Although they rejected Him, Jesus' arms are open to any Jew who believes in Him.

Apostle Paul deems those of us who are non-Jews to be grafted into the family of God (Romans 11:11-24). Gentiles were on the outside until Jesus bought our freedom and made us sons of God. Just like Moses and the children of Israel, we have not done anything to deserve this. We are not perfect! It has been given to us freely by Jesus, and now that it has been given, we have as much rights to God as any Israelite, including Abraham, Isaac, Jacob and Moses. This is truly a great honour but it comes with a warning.

Just as Moses did not enter into the promised land and just as the children of Israel who forsook Jesus will not be allowed entrance into the Kingdom of Heaven, so too will be our portion if we do not follow the commandments of God. God loves us dearly. His love for us cannot be fathomed. Jesus, out of His abundant love for us, gave up His place with God and humbled Himself, became as a poor servant, and died in our place. Despite all of this love for us, if we make mistakes in judgment by not following God like they did, our outcome will be the same. We will not enter into the Kingdom of Heaven.

Moses had another Kingdom to look forward to. He will inherit the Kingdom of Heaven. Unfortunately, those of us today who reject Jesus have no more inheritance to look forward to when He rejects us. We have no more options to be and live with God. This is the final curtain; no more dress rehearsals. We have to make good our time on earth.

The only way to ensure your place in the Kingdom is to follow God's commandments. Through your daily living, allow God's Kingdom to come into your life on earth, as it is in Heaven.

Chapter 2

Kingdom Birth (Formative Years)

Lavette and I don't have children of our own, but we took legal guardianship over our grandniece A'Mya from she was 2. She's seven now, and a handful. We don't need a psychiatrist to tell us how quickly a child develops during those early years. We have seen the changes first-hand. One day she's our little cutie pie who depends on us for everything. The next, she believes she knows more than we do. We want to teach her everything she needs, but we know that her mind cannot handle all of it. So, we wait; and for what? Before we know it, someone else is trying to frame her mindset in ways that we don't agree with. Then we are faced with the challenge of having to undo some of the nonsense she has been exposed to through insensitive adults, TV, and her little friends. The problem is that sometimes, the first message could leave indelible imprints on her mind, more so than we even understand. If only we could prevent those bad messages from ever getting to her.

Countries face similar challenges. Every successful nation tries to guard its history passionately for its identity, sovereignty, and its future. If we don't know our past, we will eventually lose our identity. If we lose our identity, we will eventually lose our heritage. If we lose our heritage, we will eventually lose our independence. And if we lose our independence, we will lose control over our future. Our past is the starting position for our future, and therefore, they are inextricably linked. **The more attuned we are to our past, the better we can shape our future**. For its sheer survival, every nation must, therefore, have a good national program to educate its citizens on its history and identity.

Some countries have national identities that are almost intrinsic to their makeup. When the goatskin drums, cowbells, horns, and whistles ring up a Junkanoo beat, Bahamians can hardly resist its allure. Junkanoo is a renowned national cultural festival in The Bahamas (my home), and most Bahamians will tell you that the music touches the core of our souls. Junkanoo is a part of who we are. Bahamians often say that there are three things you "don't get in" (in Bahamian dialect, this means "don't interfere with"); Bahamians and their religion, their politics, and their Junkanoo.

Such national symbols exist and are important in every nation. To Canadians, it might be the red Maple Leaf. To Americans, it might be the Statue of Liberty. We know that every country swells with national pride for their respective flags and national anthems. To Christians, it might be the cross.

Teaching Christians the truth about our Kingdom history is vital to our spiritual growth and survival. Our enemy has skillfully developed his ability to deceive us. From the beginning, Satan's craftiness was on full display in Eden. He played on Eve's human weaknesses and twisted God's word to eventually deceive her. He tried the same thing, though unsuccessfully, with Jesus when he tempted Him in the wilderness after Jesus fasted for 40 days. He tries the same thing with us, and because our spiritual minds have not matured, we are like Eve and A'Mya, susceptible to all sorts of error doctrines. Like both of them, we want to consume knowledge, success, and greatness in this world, but unbeknownst to us, this often comes at a very high price. According to Jesus, "whosoever will save his life shall lose it: and whosoever will lose his life for my sake shall find it." (Matthew 16:25 KJV). **When we lose our earthly lives for Jesus' sake, that's when we find our true Kingdom identity**, but too many of us are busy focusing on earth at the expense of heaven.

Our Kingdom identity is not passed down by birth. Christians hail from all over the world and have vastly varying cultures, as the nations from which we are born or live. Although there is one Kingdom of God, it has no physical boundaries. Jesus alluded to this in the Gospel of John:

> *John 18: 35-36 (KJV)* *[35]Pilate answered, Am I a Jew? Thine own nation and the chief priests have delivered thee unto me: what hast thou done? [36]Jesus answered, <u>My kingdom is not of this world: if my kingdom were of this world, then would my servants fight, that I should not be delivered to the Jews: but now is my kingdom not from hence.</u>*

His Kingdom is not of this world! John was confident about this. In the Gospel of John chapter 1:13, John said that Kingdom citizenship is not by blood–i.e., birth. What we get from birth is more in direct opposition to our Kingdom identity. We inherit a sinful nature upon birth rather than a Godly disposition.

Instead, **Kingdom citizenship is a choice** rather than a tribal bestowal of rights and privileges. Because of this, there is no coordinated national educational curriculum for Kingdom citizens. Neither is our Kingdom identity founded by norms that we have established and passed down over our history. Rather, they are based upon patterns of behaviour that God has instituted, in His wisdom and sovereignty, as to what His Kingdom will be like. These ideals have been passed down to us and enshrined in the Bible. It catalogues "national" heroes who depict the qualities that we are to elicit from ourselves, the chief example being the one King that we have and ever will have, Jesus. If we choose to become children of God, we must assume His identity, because His identity is consistent with God's. If we desire to be a part of His Kingdom, we must take on His character. If we want to accept His promises, we must portray His image.

In the first chapter of This Book, we made the connection between Grace and Truth and the Kingdom of Heaven. We also showed how the Mosaic Laws helped establish the kingdom of Israel while the Christic Laws of Liberty (Grace and Truth) are the Laws that we must follow in order to inherit or gain access into the Kingdom of Heaven. Now, we turn our attention to the birth of the Kingdom, and the prerequisites needed to enter therein.

Image of God

To understand our identity, we must trace our history all the way back to the beginning of the human race, as recorded in the Bible. There, we are told that God made man in His image, "in the image of God created He him; male and female created He them" (Genesis 1:27). Naturally, we understand that because God is a spirit, this reference to **His image** means something other than man's physical stature. He made us flesh and blood to prove this point. It's also not about our intellect since man was not yet fully aware of what sin was and what it was not. Intellectually, we were babes, ignorant even of good and evil. At seven years old, our darling A'Mya can tell the difference. God did not give man eternal life at that point, either. So, it wasn't His omnipresence that defined this relationship with God. It's my contention that **the image of God was referring to God's nature**, i.e., His persona, instead.

What really differentiated man from all other creatures that God created was that man was made in God's image and likeness. This distinction was important to God, which led Him to give us dominion over the earth. Contrary to what we might hear elsewhere, **man's dominion over the earth is more of a privilege of living in God's image than the purpose of being man.** We know this because when God became angry with the sinful nature of man, He was prepared to totally remove us from the earth over which He gave us dominion. According to Genesis 6:5-6, God became terribly disappointed that He made man, as a result of the evil in man's heart. Man had departed from God's image. They were still the same physically; they were multiplying on the earth as He commanded; they were growing intellectually; they still had dominion on the earth. Despite all of these, man was not fulfilling God's original plan for their lives, and He was very disappointed, even angry, with them. Do you remember when Jesus cursed the fig tree because it did not have any fruit on it? Likewise, God had enough of mankind's unfruitfulness because they no longer walked in His image, and He decided to destroy man, just as He did the unfruitful fig tree. Once evil took root in man, God's image, which was what God wanted to see in man, was no longer visible.

Noah, on the other hand, was different. Noah remained "just and perfect" (Genesis 6:9), and because of this, he found grace in the eyes of God. Noah continued to walk in the image of God. God, therefore, saved Noah when He destroyed everyone else in the flood. When it all boils down, God still wants man to live in His image and in His likeness. Those who do will be saved just as godly Noah was saved. Those who do not will ultimately be cast away from God, just like those who perished in the flood.

God's intent was that man would develop the earth and create offspring in man's image, which, by extension, would be in God's image as long as man maintained his relationship with God. This is why the Bible says in Genesis 5:3 that Adam begat a son (Seth) in his own likeness and image. This, I believe, is how we become fruitful as God commanded Adam.

Failure to maintain God's image is sin. When we fail to keep God's image, it separates us from God. God told Adam and Eve that they would die the day that they ate of the tree of knowledge of good and evil. If they sinned, by disobeying God, they would be separated from Him unto death.

Inside Out

By referencing His image and likeness in Genesis 1:26, God's intention was always for man to place a high priority on the things that He saw as important. He wanted us to pursue His attributes–mercy, kindness, and love. In our ignorance, however, mankind has substituted these pure qualities of God for religious rituals and dogma, which prioritised an outward-in focus. God, instead, has always wanted us to focus from the **inside-out**. Micah 6:8 says that there are three things that God requires of man:

1. To do justly

2. To love mercy

3. To walk humbly with our God

All of these characteristics look from the inside, where the heart is, and projects to the outside, toward others. Doing justly means showing impartiality to others. It starts from the inside of us and launches fairness to others. Mercy is the act of showing sympathy and compassion to others. It also starts within and is directed outwardly. Walking humbly with God means yielding our personal will and desires to God. Again, it starts within, with humility, and projects outwardly toward God.

In the preamble of this section, we talked about how God used Moses to usher in the Era of God's Divine Nature. In Exodus 33:18, Moses asked God to reveal Himself to him. At first glance, it appears that Moses wanted to see some physical manifestation of God. However, given the miraculous experiences that Moses had with God, combined with God's response to Moses, I am sure that Moses was not asking for a physical manifestation of God. He was asking God for a better comprehension of who He is.

In Exodus 6:3, even before God delivered the Hebrews from Egypt, God mentioned to Moses that He is the Lord. He also helped Moses see that He was entering a new phase with mankind, one in which they would get a better understanding of who He is. This is what He said to Moses:

Exodus 6:2-3 (KJV) ²And God spake unto Moses, and said unto him, I am the Lord: ³And I appeared unto Abraham, unto Isaac, and unto Jacob, by the name of God Almighty, but by my name Jehovah was I not known to them.

The Common English Bible version puts the same scripture this way:

Exodus 6:2-3 (CEB) ²God also said to Moses: "I am the Lord. ³I appeared to Abraham, Isaac, and Jacob as God Almighty, but I didn't reveal myself to them by my name 'The Lord.'..."

As time passed, Moses experienced the power of God when He delivered them out of Egypt. Moses also got to see God multiple times; once when he specifically led the children of Israel out of their camp to meet with God:

Exodus 19:17-18 (KJV) ¹⁷And Moses brought forth the people out of the camp <u>to meet with God</u>; they stood at the nether part of the mount. ¹⁸And mount Sinai was altogether on a smoke, because <u>the Lord descended upon it in fire</u>: and the smoke thereof ascended as the smoke of a furnace, and the whole mount quaked greatly.

By most definitions, this experience was the glory of God. It happened another time. If the previous scripture wasn't clear enough, perhaps this one will do the trick.

*Exodus 24:15-18 (KJV) ¹⁵And Moses went up into the mount, and a cloud covered the mount. ¹⁶And the glory of the Lord abode upon mount Sinai and the cloud covered it six days: and the seventh day he called unto Moses out of the midst of the cloud. ¹⁷And <u>**the sight of the glory of the Lord was like devouring fire on the top of the mount**</u> in the eyes of the children of Israel. ¹⁸And Moses went into the midst of the cloud, and gat him up into the mount: and Moses was in the mount forty days and forty nights.*

Moses definitely had seen the glory of God. This is why we can be sure that he was asking God to show him something different; he wanted to understand who God is. In Exodus 33:13, just before the conversation about seeing the glory of God, Moses explicitly expressed his interests. Here's what he said:

¹³Now, therefore, I pray thee, if I have found grace in thy sight, <u>shew me now thy way, that I may know thee, that I may find grace in thy sight</u>: and consider that this nation is thy people.

Moses wanted to know God and understand God's ways. To Moses, this was how he could be assured of pleasing God. The Common English Bible version interprets the above scripture this way:

(CEB) ¹³Now, if you do think highly of me, <u>show me your ways so that I may know you and so that you may really approve of me</u>. Remember too that this nation is your people.

God's response to the question about His Glory in Exodus 33:18 was to make all His goodness pass before Moses. Then, in verse 19, He said these unusual words under the circumstance, "I will proclaim the name of the Lord before thee; and will be gracious to whom I will be gracious, and will shew mercy on whom I will shew mercy." God was ushering in a new era wherein people would know Him by His name, "The Lord."

God promised to reveal Himself to Moses, and He did. It is recorded in Exodus 34:1-7. When God revealed Himself, He reiterated loudly and clearly exactly who He is in Exodus 34:6b-7:

> *6bThe Lord, The Lord God, merciful and gracious, longsuffering, and abundant in goodness and truth, 7Keeping mercy for thousands, forgiving iniquity and transgression and sin, and that will by no means clear the guilty; visiting the iniquity of the fathers upon the children, and upon the children's children, unto the third and fourth generation.*

This monolog encapsulates everything we need to know about God. **This is who He is! This is His nature! This is His image!** First of all, it depicts His sovereignty. He is the Lord, and to be clear, He repeated who He is and added the name "God"! He is the Lord God! He is:

- Creator of the world

- Omnipotent–All-powerful

- Omnipresent–everywhere at the same time

- Omniscient–Knows everything

- Eternal–No beginning or end to His existence

- Immutable–Does not change

- Sovereign–His will is supreme

- Transcendent–Not subject to time and space

And despite His superiority to any and everything, He is nonetheless inward-out looking. He is unselfish. He is merciful. He is gracious. He has an abundance of goodness and is honest and forgiving. He can exercise His abundance of power, yet he decides to be merciful, good, and kind. He is also fair. He will not clear the guilty, and He will punish sin. Those of us who, like a cloak, try to use God's loving-kindness and tender mercies to cover themselves from His ultimate judgment and punishment against sin, will be sadly awakened to the day they face His judgment. Read His lips! He will "by no means clear the guilty."

Based on this, are we still living according to God's image today? Do we prioritise mercy, justice, and humility? Do we love God with all our heart, soul, mind, and strength? Despite what power and authority we may possess on earth, do we humble ourselves? These are personal questions that each of us must answer. But I fear that even among Christians today, there has been a slow drift away from these attributes and a gradual drawing toward wealth, success, excellence, winning, etc.; which things encourage self-gratification, self-confidence, and personal growth and development–things that make Self better and are good for the individual, but which leads us down a selfish path. Meanwhile, **God is asking us to keep our selfishness confined, and to humble our desires to Him and to His will, looking outward toward others.** Of course, we may concurrently pursue our personal interests, but not selfishly, that is, not where we injure, cheat, harm, disregard, disrespect, or defraud others, and certainly not where we prioritize them over our relationship with God.

In 2 Timothy 3:1, the Bible says that in the last days, perilous times will come. Right out the gate, Paul gave his definition of, or perhaps his reasons for, perilous times, and among the first things he refers to are that men shall be "lovers of their own selves, covetous, boasters, proud," things that promote self. A few verses later, Paul finishes his list with "heady, highminded, lovers of pleasures more than lovers of God," things that look outward for inward gratification. These things, Paul thought, would cause great peril to mankind.

Unfortunately, our gospel message today encourages a lot of self-promotion. Listen carefully, and you too might agree that many of them promote the Self. It's as if many preachers have become personal development coaches and motivational speakers. Even the messages that start out teaching us that we may have to suffer some difficulties and setbacks in life usually ends with us being told that we will soon (that is, in this life), get everything that we want. The crux of the message being that any suffering that we experience are only prerequisites for abundant blessings and rewards here and soon. The subtle nuance of this is that it shifts the focus away from suffering for Christ's sake to suffering for our reward. This is an outward-in focus, rather than an inward-out one.

We, as humans, like to "get," and many times, we put ourselves in competition against others for the limited resources of this world. After all, we all can't become Prime Minister or President. We all can't win in a race no more than we can all get the promotion on the job. We all can't be first, no matter how much we are told God wants us to be first and not last. We all want the best things for ourselves, but oftentimes when we get it, the sad reality is that someone else may be deprived. That does not stop us. In fact, it seems to motivate us to ensure we are never the ones being deprived. God, on the other hand, is a giving God, and He has a different perspective on relationship priorities than we typically do. His hierarchy looks something like this:

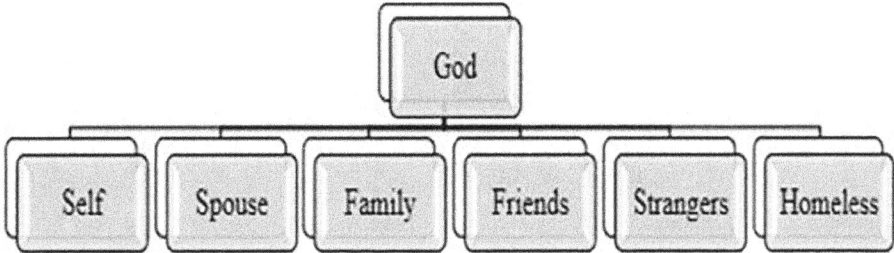

God must be above all, and everyone else at the same level in terms of importance or priority. But most of us have Self above at least one of these groups, and sadly, some of us have put self above all of these other groups. Jesus taught us to love our neighbour <u>as ourselves</u>, and his definition of neighbour includes each of these other groups and more. If it's true that we prioritize ourselves above others, i.e., that we are outward-in looking and/or selfish, Jesus wants us to repent because we would not be living in His image nor following God's standards of humility and meekness.

Death by sin

Adam and Eve were the first to choose to stop living in the image of God. Despite being warned by God that they would die if they did not keep His one commandment, they still sinned against Him. Adam's sin was disobedience. God told him, "for in the day that thou eatest thereof thou shalt surely die" (Genesis 2:17). Death, therefore, became Adam's punishment for disobeying God, and according to Romans 5 (below), Adam's death was transferred to the rest of us who sinned.

12Wherefore, as by one man sin entered into the world, and death by sin; and so death passed upon all men, for that all have sinned:

Houston…we have a big problem! God's majestic creation had to die.

Sin still has the same effect today. If we sin against God, we cannot be with Him. **Death is the only alternative that we have when we choose not to follow God.**

But glory be to God that He is loving and merciful by nature. He did not leave us in that condition but paved the way for our deliverance from sin and death.

God had a plan!

He decided that in order to save mankind from certain death, He would do it through a man. This is what God foreshadowed when he cursed the serpent in Genesis chapter 3.

> *Genesis 3:14-15 (KJV) [14]And the Lord God said unto the serpent, Because thou hast done this, thou art cursed above all cattle, and above every beast of the field; upon thy belly shalt thou go, and dust shalt thou eat all the days of thy life: [15]And I will put enmity between thee and the woman, and between thy seed and her seed; it shall bruise thy head, and thou shalt bruise his heel.*

This is the first prophesy about Jesus and the eventual victory He will bring to His people. It's also the first prophesy about the looming destruction of the devil and his cohorts, including people who choose not to align themselves with Jesus. God had a plan from day one, and He knew it could only be filled by someone greater than His enemy (Lucifer). That's why He sent His only Son to take on the form of a human (seed of the woman) and to defeat the devil. The irony is that God chose to re-establish man's relationship with Him through the same vehicle that originally divided us from Him. Mankind lost our place with God because we did not heed to His commandments. It is through keeping His commandments that we are restored in full relationship with Him. Here's how Jesus put it:

> *John 14:21-23 (KJV) [21]He that hath my commandments, and keepeth them, he it is that loveth me: and he that loveth me shall be loved of my Father, and I will love him, and will manifest myself to him. [22]Judas saith unto him, not Iscariot, Lord, how is it that thou wilt manifest thyself unto us, and not unto the world? [23]Jesus answered and said unto him, If a man love me, he will keep my words: and my Father will love him, and we will come unto him, and make our abode with him.*

This is one of the few times that Jesus spoke in parables, then immediately explained Himself. He said that He would manifest Himself to anyone who loves Him and keeps His commandments. Judas asked Him to clarify what he meant, and He explained that God and He will make their abode with those of us who keep His commandments. In other words, we will be restored to the kind of relationship Adam and Eve had with God before they sinned against Him, back to His image and likeness.

Father Abraham

The fact that God's Son would have to be human created a mammoth challenge. Since God elected to send His Son to earth as a human, invariably, He had to choose from among all of the different tribes and nationalities on the earth, which line His Son would come from. They were all sinful and, therefore, for all intents and purposes, "dead." Roman 5:14 says, "Nevertheless death reigned from Adam to Moses, even over them that had not sinned after the similitude of Adam's transgression." Because it was important to God to save mankind, He had to choose from whose lineage the Saviour would come, regardless of the unworthiness of every human on earth. God chose undeserving Abram!

It is indeed a great honour to be chosen by God for any reason, but for this, to be chosen as the father of the Son of God, the honour is immeasurable. When God called Abraham, he made certain representations (or promises) to him, including that he would be a great nation. At the time of his calling, Abram was just a part of a large, relatively rich family. He (they) was not a nation...not even close.

Genesis 12:1-3 (KJV) Now the Lord had said unto Abram, Get thee out of thy country, and from thy kindred, and from thy father's house, unto a land that I will shew thee: ²And I will make of thee a great nation, and I will bless thee, and make thy name great; and thou shalt be a blessing: ³And I will bless them that bless thee, and curse him that curseth thee: and in thee shall all families of the earth be blessed.

At this point, Abram had done nothing to earn this honour. In fact, Abram's father, Terah, was a polytheist. That's why God called Abram **away** from his country, his father, his kindred and away from their false gods. In order to redevelop him into God's image, Abram had to be purged from his ancestral propensities. It was God's predestined choice, early evidence of His mercy and grace, to call a man to such high honour who had not done anything to deserve it, much the way He gives us all grace and mercy to call us "while we were yet sinners" (Roman 5:8).

The Bible says that Abraham believed God, and it was accounted to him for righteousness. This signifies that Abraham was not called because of his own worthiness, but because of his faith. We, too, can walk closely with God by having faith. Conversely, this also means that we cannot please God without faith, no more than we can please Him through our own righteousness, or by the deeds of our flesh.

Abraham was definitely not perfect, and despite our predisposition, his faith was not always impressive. After God told Abraham that He would give him the land of Canaan, Abraham, displaying a modicum of doubt, immediately asked God for proof that He would do it.

Genesis 15:5-8 (KJV) 5And he brought him forth abroad, and said, Look now toward heaven, and tell the stars, if thou be able to number them: and he said unto him, So shall thy seed be. 6And he believed in the Lord; and he counted it to him for righteousness. 7And he said unto him, I am the Lord that brought thee out of Ur of the Chaldees, to give thee this land to inherit it. 8And he said, Lord God, whereby shall I know that I shall inherit it?

The fact that he asked God for proof of His promise shows a level of distrust. Despite the weakness of his humanity, we know that Abram persisted in his belief of God, and it was because of this that he was justified by God. God overlooked his frailties because he ultimately kept his faith and followed after God. Abram, therefore, displayed God's image by having faith–as it is written, "without faith, it is impossible to please him" (Hebrews 11:6).

Abraham did not personally inherit the land because the promise really was about a heavenly land, which will be the reward of all who, like Abraham, maintains our faith in God. In this respect, we are not very different from Abraham. We believe in God and know that He is supreme. Yet, we have lots of doubt when it comes to His omnipotence, particularly regarding things that are difficult to see. But through the example of Abraham, God is telling us to hold fast to our faith in Him, and that He will ultimately reward us, not necessarily in this life, but like Abraham, in the Kingdom to come.

Because God decided to establish his blessings through Abram, He changed his name to Abraham, signifying newness. Abram was still Abram, but Abraham was something different. Abram was physical, but Abraham was spiritual, faith-filled, made in God's image. God wanted to pave the way for His Son through a spiritual line, not of blood. Abram was the son of man named by his earthly father, Terah, but Abraham was the son of God, named by his heavenly Father Jehovah.

Genesis 17:5 (KJV) Neither shall thy name any more be called Abram, but thy name shall be Abraham; for a father of many nations have I made thee.

The significance was that Abraham foreshadowed Jesus. It's through Jesus, not Abraham, that all nations of the earth would be blessed. Jesus is the father of many nations–Jews and Gentiles, "For as many as believed on Him, gave he power to become the **Sons of God.**"

Abram's fleshly lineage included his son Isaac whom God used to confirm (some might say test) Abram's complete obedience to God. After Abraham proved his dedication, God affirmed his blessing to Abraham and to his people:

Genesis 22:16-18 (KJV) 16And said, By myself have I sworn, saith the Lord, for because thou hast done this thing, and hast not withheld thy son, thine only son: 17That in blessing I will bless thee, and in multiplying I will multiply thy seed as the stars of the heaven, and as the sand which is upon the sea shore; and thy seed shall possess the gate of his enemies; 18And in thy seed shall all the nations of the earth be blessed; because thou hast obeyed my voice.

God distinguished that not in the man Abraham would all the nations of the earth be blessed, but in his seed. This seed is Jesus Christ. Our blessings are not from Abraham, nor from Israel, and they're not from The Bahamas. No, they're not from America, China, France, Russia, Brazil, Britain, or any of the other countries of the world. They're through Jesus! Paul affirmed this in his letter to the Galatians.

Galatians 3:16 (KJV) Now to Abraham and his seed were the promises made. He saith not, And to seeds, as of many; but as of one, And to thy seed, which is Christ.

This is reaffirmed in Romans.

Romans 4:13-16 (KJV) 13For the promise, that he should be the heir of the world, was not to Abraham, or to his seed, through the law, but through the righteousness of faith. 14For if they which are of the law be heirs, faith is made void, and the promise made of none effect: 15Because the law worketh wrath: for where no law is, there is no transgression. 16Therefore it is of faith, that it might be by grace; to the end the promise might be sure to all the seed; not to that only which is of the law, but to that also which is of the faith of Abraham; who is the father of us all,

Ultimately, everything about Abraham was symbolic of something greater. Abraham was justified by his faith, because through faith, would we all be justified. Everything promised to Abraham was meant to explain what we all would have through faith. **The promises were never really about Abraham or his natural seed. It was always meant for everyone who has faith in God and who, through that faith, would live in God's image.** Since the seed was not the seed according to the law, it is reasonable to think that despite the ongoing rumbling and fighting about Jerusalem, **the promised land was never about the land that the law seed would eventually possess. It was and is about the land that the faith seed will possess. It is about Heaven.** Their promised land was only a microcosm of what the true promised land would be.

Trouble foretold

When God promised Abraham that his seed would be innumerable, He did something quite strange. He simultaneously promised him hardship and suffering for his seed. Abraham, like his descendants, seemed to think that God was making a pact with his natural seed. It is highly unusual, to say the least, that God would make a promise to Abraham that he would possess the land, then immediately tell him that for 400 years, his descendants would live in a strange land and suffer oppression under the hands of a different nation.

> *Genesis 15:13-14 (KJV)* *[13]And he said unto Abram, Know of a surety that thy seed shall be a stranger in a land that is not theirs, <u>and shall serve them; and they shall afflict them four hundred years;</u> [14]And also that nation, whom they shall serve, will I judge: and afterward shall they come out with great substance.*

It was through Moses that this deliverance foretold in verse 14 came to pass 400 years later.

Kingdom of Israel

After God delivered the children of Israel from the bondage of the Egyptians, He established Israel as a nation by giving them laws (ten commandments and other laws) and land (Canaan and neighbouring cities). A new kingdom was coming. Finally, God would make them a nation and, eventually, a kingdom.

Moses was trained as a high-ranking Egyptian. We know his story well, how he was protected by his mother when Pharaoh decreed that all Hebrew children of a certain age must be killed because the Hebrew population grew too much. Of course, the Hebrews were the Israelites, and Moses was one of them. Pharaoh's daughter saw baby Moses in the river and decided to keep him and raise him as her son. Moses, therefore, grew up along with the close relatives of Pharaoh, which meant that he was trained and educated in the inner working of Egyptian governments, laws, leadership, etc. This would eventually prove both beneficial and costly.

When they left Egypt, Moses was given the ten commandments by God to deliver and teach to the children of Israel. However, Moses gave them many other laws and statutes, some commanded by God and some not; some written and others oral; some were even developed over time by their Elders. The benefit of the Laws was designed to help this new nation of Israel become organized and structured. The ultimate intent was to re-establish God's image in His people. The Laws were intended to show them how to live for God.

But there was a cost. The Laws became a source of weaponry against the people, as so many rules were punishable by death. It paved the way for the ritualistic following of rules and regulations rather than righteousness as God intended.

Hear Jesus

While Moses was a great prophet within the kingdom of Israel, his role was pale compared to Jesus and the Kingdom of Heaven. The Israelites had elevated Moses and the prophets within their nation. However, in the transfiguration of Jesus, a clear message lingered, that Jesus was above Moses and the prophets, and stood alone as the Chosen One.

Mark 9:2-8 (KJV) [2]And after six days Jesus taketh with him Peter, and James, and John, and leadeth them up into an high mountain apart by themselves: and he was transfigured before them. [3]And his raiment became shining, exceeding white as snow; so as no fuller on earth can white them. [4]And there appeared unto them Elias with Moses: and they were talking with Jesus. [5]And Peter answered and said to Jesus, Master, it is good for us to be here: and let us make three tabernacles; one for thee, and one for Moses, and one for Elias. [6]For he wist not what to say; for they were sore afraid. [7]And there was a cloud that overshadowed them: and a voice came out of the cloud, saying, This is my beloved Son: hear him. [8]And suddenly, when they had looked round about, they saw no man any more, save Jesus only with themselves.

It is through Jesus that the Kingdom would be established, not through Moses, nor through the prophets.

*Isaiah 9:6-7 (KJV) ⁶For unto us a child is born, unto us a son is given: and the government shall be upon his shoulder: and his name shall be called Wonderful, Counsellor, The mighty God, The everlasting Father, The Prince of Peace. ⁷Of the increase of his government and **peace**there shall be no end, upon the throne of David, and upon his kingdom, to order it, and to establish it with **judgment**and with **justice** from henceforth even for ever. The zeal of the Lord of hosts will perform this.*

This prophecy was about Jesus, the Son of God, and His Kingdom of peace, judgment, and justice (yes, the image of God!). The kingdom of Israel was already established when this prophecy was foretold. Therefore, this prophesy was actually about another kingdom that was yet to come. Jesus fulfilled this when He preached that the Kingdom of Heaven was at hand, the true Kingdom which God foretold when referring to Abraham as the father of many nations.

As part of His deliverance of the Hebrews from Egypt, God ushered in a new revelation of Himself. Previously, He was not known by His name "The Lord" or Jehovah. He revealed His name to and through Moses. Likewise, through Jesus, God ushered in a new revelation of who He is (i.e., His name). He ushered in Grace and Truth, the avenue to restore us to God's image.

Christ came to earth and showed us how to live according to God's image. John's Gospel (1:4-5) states, "In him was life, and the life was the light of men. And the light shineth in darkness; and the darkness comprehended it not." His life is the light, or example, for us to see and follow. The world is in darkness. Not physically, but spiritually. Our eyes are blinded, also spiritually. But not all of us. In 2 Corinthians 4:3-4, Paul summarises this exact dialog by connecting the light of Jesus with the "image of God."

*2 Corinthians 4:3-4 (KJV) ³But if our gospel be hid, it is hid to them that are lost: ⁴In whom the god of this world hath blinded the minds of them which believe not, lest the light of the glorious gospel of Christ, **who is the image of God**, should shine unto them.*

By giving us Grace and Truth, Jesus re-defined how we are supposed to live in God's image, thus taking us back to our original place as God intended. The hyphen is used in the word re-defined as a play on words. Jesus redefined it, but only by re-establishing something that existed previously. It was God's original plan for man to be made in His image. Jesus created the avenue for us to get back on track.

PERSONAL APPLICATION
GRACE VS. LONG SUFFERING

In His own words, God defined His character. He is merciful, gracious, longsuffering, and abundant in goodness and truth (Exodus 34:6). These traits are very similar, but two of them in particular look so much the same, that they have often been confused with each other—grace and longsuffering.

Merriam-Webster defines Grace as "unmerited divine assistance given to humans for their regeneration or sanctification." Christians commonly call it "God's unmerited favour to man." We explain God's grace as the thing that cleanses our sins. It blots them away. Makes us new people, as if we never sinned before.

Grace is also something that has the power over any sin (with the exception of the unpardonable sins, e.g. blasphemy against the Holy Spirit). The Bible says where sin abounds, grace did much more abound (Romans 5:20). The vision of grace is something that covers all sins and makes us right with God. It does not matter how much we sin, grace covers it.

However, the Bible also asks "Shall we continue to sin that grace may abound? God forbid. How shall we, that are dead to sin, live any longer therein?" (Romans 6:1-2). Notice the confusion? On the one hand, grace covers all sins, but on the other hand, we cannot continue to sin because of grace. The fine line between these points is called longsuffering.

Longsuffering is God's patience toward our sins and disobedience. He allows us to sin and sin and sin, doing the same things, making the same mistakes, over and over again. And He does not punish us for it. He continues to bless us, protect us, love us, promote us on the job, give us favour, keep us from harm and injury. His longsuffering allows us to keep sinning without penalty. When we think about it, longsuffering looks like grace...but it isn't the same.

The devil has caused us to confuse longsuffering with grace. He makes us believe that we can continue to sin and it will be okay because of God's grace. He points to the fact that God still blesses us even when we sin and this is what sells us on the notion that we can continue to sin because of grace. However, when we say this, we are confusing longsuffering with grace. What is the implication? Why is this important? It's because grace covers sin, but longsuffering does not. Longsuffering only forbears sin. In other words, with grace, sin is gone entirely, but with longsuffering, sin remains.

Paul didn't want us to get confused with the two which is why he penned those words in Romans 6:1-2. He said "God forbid" to the notion that we can continue to sin because we have grace to cover us. He suggests that grace makes us dead to sin, and since we are dead to it, we can't live in sin anymore. When we continue to sin, we are not dead to it, which means the sin has not been removed.

In His description of His character, God indicates that He will not clear the guilty (Exodus 34:7). This means that unless sin has been removed (or cleared), we will be convicted (as in a court of law), and we will suffer the penalty of sin, which is death. Longsuffering does not clear sin, but its effect closely resembles grace. Confusing longsuffering with grace in this way is a most colossal mistake that will lead to our demise. The Bible says that the goodness of God leads us to repentance. But some of us think it leads us to continue sinning. That's unfortunate because so much is at stake. Until sin is killed by grace, that is, until we STOP repeating the same sin over and over, God continues to be longsuffering toward us, but the sin remains in us. While the sin remains, we are holding on to a rope which has an end to it. Eventually, it will lead to that part of God's nature that will not clear the guilty.

Brothers and sisters, let us learn the difference between grace and longsuffering and that God's goodness is not evidence of His grace, but of His longsuffering. His longsuffering does not clear our sins.

Chapter 3

Kingdom Prerequisites (Repentance & Baptism)

Something's wrong

When Jesus first preached about the Kingdom, he called for repentance as a prerequisite for the Kingdom. Repent, He said, for the Kingdom is at hand. By these words, particularly the use of REPENT, Jesus was signifying that He saw something materially different in the lives of the people from what God desired of them. In some significant way, the people were not aligned with God. They were still not living in God's image.

Consider that at this time, Mosaic Laws had been established. The priesthood was fully operational and the religious leaders were in full force and effect. There were educated scholars (scribes and lawyers) whose primary function was to interpret the Laws and thereby ensure that the Jews kept strict adherence to the statutes and principles of God. Nevertheless, something was amiss. Jesus saw something missing from their lives.

But what did Jesus see that was wrong? He saw people who had disfigured and forced God's original and lasting intent for righteous and holy living, into manmade religion, which left off the meatier things, the important things that God expected from us. The Laws became a tool of death and bondage rather than a life-giving and liberating force to return the heart and soul of man back to the image of God.

Many of the Laws given by Moses had the penalty of death, but none could give life, as confirmed in Galatians 3:21. Moses was fed up with the infidelity of his people and he wanted to make it difficult for them to forsake God again. He was right about them because they regularly disobeyed God and went after "strange gods." The punishment of death in the many Laws was symbolic of the death penalty for sin. Paul put it this way:

Romans 7:9-12 (KJV) ⁹For I was alive without the law once: but when the commandment came, sin revived, and I died. ¹⁰And the commandment, which was ordained to life, I found to be unto death. ¹¹For sin, taking occasion by the commandment, deceived me, and by it slew me. ¹²Wherefore the law is holy, and the commandment holy, and just, and good.

Instead of death, Jesus came to give us the abundant life that the Laws could not give (John 10:10). We can only have eternal life by Jesus if we keep His righteousness, that is, if we keep **His** commandments. But before righteousness comes repentance.

Repent

Just before they inherited the promised land, the original Hebrew men and women that God delivered from Egypt by the hands of Moses were pretty much all dead (other than a few of them). Moses wanting to teach the new generation about God introduced new laws in Deuteronomy that were not included in the original laws that God gave to him. Deuteronomy is the last book of the Torah (i.e. first five books of the Bible generally attributed to Moses), and it literally means "second law", derived from the Greek words deuteros and nomos. Besides these, other laws were developed over time, having been passed down from the Elders. Some of the Laws were written and others were Oral.

The Jews took the Laws and traditions seriously. They felt that their traditions were aligned with God and because of this, they used their traditions as a barometer to determine those who were in step with God and those who were not. Those deemed out of line were to be punished according to the Laws and traditions. Perhaps because they didn't fully understand them, or perhaps because they sought to justify themselves, their traditions ran afoul of what God intended. Despite their attempts to fashion the Laws of Moses and the traditions of their forefathers to the will and intent of God, Jesus understood that their lives, especially that of the religious leaders, were in conflict with the image of God. They had to repent!

Repent means to change. Jesus' message to the Jews was that they needed to change, notwithstanding their compliance with the traditions of their fathers. Here is what Jesus said about their traditions:

Mark 7:5-13 (KJV) ⁵Then the Pharisees and scribes asked him, Why walk not thy disciples according to the tradition of the elders, but eat bread with unwashen hands? ⁶He answered and said unto them, Well hath Esaias prophesied of you hypocrites, as it is written, This people honoureth me with their lips, but their heart is far from me. [7]Howbeit in vain do they worship me, teaching for doctrines the commandments of men. [8]For laying aside the commandment of God, ye hold the tradition of men, as the washing of pots and cups: and many other such like things ye do. [9]And he said unto them, Full well ye reject the commandment of God, that ye may keep your own tradition. [10]For Moses said, Honour thy father and thy mother; and, Whoso curseth father or mother, let him die the death: [11]But ye say, If a man shall say to his father or mother, It is Corban, that is to say, a gift, by whatsoever thou mightest be profited by me; he shall be free. [12]And ye suffer him no more to do ought for his father or his mother; [13]Making the word of God of none effect through your tradition, which ye have delivered: and many such like things do ye.

These are strong words that Jesus had about the Pharisees and the traditions of their Elders. As part of the religious movement against Hellenization (that is, indoctrination of the Greeks into Jewish culture), the Pharisees felt that they were committed to the original Mosaic Laws, the interpretation of which were enhanced and expanded by their forefathers. For the Pharisees, the Jews had compromised themselves by allowing the infiltration of Greek culture into their lives. They were opposed to this strongly and their movement was growing.

On the other hand, there were the Sadducees whom the Pharisees viewed as the elite believers who maintained the temple. They had very different views on the traditions, including the Oral Laws, rejecting them as inspired scripture. However, while rejecting the traditions that were promoted by the Pharisees, the Sadducees had their own traditions based on their extraordinarily strict interpretations of the Laws. They were more literal than the Pharisees in interpreting the scriptures and this too was contrary to God's will in some cases.

The question raised by the Pharisees in the above scripture appears to have been more than a concern about adherence to the traditions, in light of the conflicts between the views of these two major sects. Not only did they want Jesus to obey their rules, they appear to also have wanted Him to side with them against the Sadducees. These religious groups were the leading teachers and sects at that time, and they had scribes in both groups who devoted themselves to the doctrines of the Laws. They each demanded strict adherence to them, even at times to the death. They found the authority to kill for the Laws from Moses. In the Laws, Moses taught that they are not to have mercy on people who disobeyed the Laws. In Deuteronomy 13:8, Moses demanded this judgement against any brother, son, daughter, wife, or friend who as much as asked them to serve other gods, saying "neither shall thine eye pity him, neither shall thou spare, neither shall thou conceal him: but thou shall surely kill him." No wonder they were so comfortable crucifying Jesus for actions that they deemed to be breaking the Laws.

These religious leaders were zealots over the Laws and were ready to mete out any and all punishment enshrined in it. But Jesus was not pleased with their conduct and was intent on showing them the truth. Here are some of the harsh words He said about the religious leaders and their misguided interpretations and false adherence to Mosaic Laws.

Matthew 23:1-7 (KJV) ¹Then spake Jesus to the multitude, and to his disciples, ²Saying The scribes and the Pharisees sit in Moses' seat: ³All therefore whatsoever they bid you observe, that observe and do; but do not ye after their works: for they say, and do not. ⁴For they bind heavy burdens and grievous to be borne, and lay them on men's shoulders; but they themselves will not move them with one of their fingers. ⁵But all their works they do for to be seen of men: they make broad their phylacteries, and enlarge the borders of their garments, ⁶And love the uppermost rooms at feasts, and the chief seats in the synagogues, ⁷And greetings in the markets, and to be called of men, Rabbi, Rabbi.

Don't these things sound an awful lot like the religious leaders were self-indulgent? They were outward-in people who believed that everything should have accrued to their benefit. They could make demands of everyone else, but because of their self-righteousness, they did not need to live what they preached. Are we so different from them today? To the extent that we are alike, it's under severe penalty of rejection by Christ. Consider what Jesus said in:

Matthew 5:20 (KJV) For I say unto you, That except your righteousness shall exceed the righteousness of the scribes and Pharisees, ye shall in no case enter into the kingdom of Heaven.

From the onset, Jesus made it clear that the religious leaders were headed down the wrong path. He constantly chastised them for their incorrect interpretations of the scriptures. Just look at the examples in the most popular sermon that Jesus gave, the Kingdom Sermon on the Mount, where Jesus rejected the interpretations of the religious leaders and gave the people the correct interpretations from God.

Scripture	Religious Leaders Interpretation	Jesus's Corrections
Matt 5: 21 & 22	Thou shalt not kill	Thou shalt not be angry without a cause
Matt 5:27 & 28	Thou shall not commit adultery	Thou shall not look at a woman to lust after her
Matt 5: 31 & 32	A man may divorce after giving his wife a writing of divorcement	A man can only divorce due to fornication
Matt 5:33 & 34	Perform all oaths	Do not swear at all
Matt 5: 38 & 39	An eye for an eye	Turn the other cheek
Matt 5: 43 & 44	Love your neighbours and hate your enemies	Love your enemies and do good to them that hate you.

Jesus came, in part, to establish a new way of life, i.e. Kingdom life that conformed with the image of God. This is the life which He wanted them (and us) to change to. Move from selfishness toward unselfishness; from putting ourselves and our interests first, to putting God and His interests first; from arrogance to mercy; from putting our neighbours' needs behind ours to putting them on equal par with ours; from focusing outward-in to looking inward-out. This inward-out focus is why Jesus said that only what comes out of a man defiles him (Mark 7: 14-23). Verses 21 to 23 hone in on this message, that it is what comes from the heart that defiles us (i.e. defiles our Godly image).

Today, the world is filled with so much debauchery–murder, hatred, lust, war, prejudice, racism, and so on. These, Jesus preached, are what defiles us. They are not new maladies, but have afflicted humans since the fall of mankind. In Galatians, the Bible says that the flesh lusteth against the Spirit and the Spirit against the flesh. Then Paul continued to define the deeds of the flesh:

Galatians 5:19-21 (KJV) ¹⁹Now the works of the flesh are manifest, which are these; Adultery, fornication, uncleanness, lasciviousness, ²⁰Idolatry, witchcraft, *hatred, variance, emulations, wrath, strife, seditions, heresies, [21]Envyings, murders, drunkenness, revellings, and such like: of the which I tell you before, as I have also told you in time past, <u>that they which do such things shall not inherit the kingdom of God.</u>*

Notice the underlined text. Those of us who do those things will not inherit the Kingdom of God. If these deeds have been anything, they have been consistent throughout the world's history, and they continue to plague us today. Two things to consider here: 1) Anyone, without exception, who does these things (meaning who practises, or deliberately does them, without seeking the Spirit's help to CHANGE), will not inherit the Kingdom, and 2) Anyone who is not a part of God's kingdom, is not a part of God.

That's why Jesus made it a primary purpose of His ministry on earth to preach about repentance and the Kingdom. <u>But His message about repentance was about more than salvation, more than a religious association, more than a name by which we are recognized, and more than asking for forgiveness. It was about change. It is about change.</u> The Israelites had established something that materially differed from God's intent much the same way we have today, with our multiplicity of denominations, interpretations of the scriptures, and our doctrines, which in some cases have no scriptural reference to begin with.

We love to deride the Chief Priests, Scribes, Pharisees and Sadducees in the Bible, but I have found that we have more in common with them than we have differences. Most of our Christian denominations have theories that are akin to the Oral Laws and traditions of the Jews, stuff that have been passed down over time. Many of them ostracize individuals who are different. Most of them reject anyone with dissenting views because it's more important to maintain the standards of their historical belief systems, than to accept differences from other denominations or other people, even in the face of overwhelming supporting scriptural references.

Paul prophesied about this when he said there are differences in administration, **but the same Spirit**. If only we would appreciate that there are no distinguishable differences between us when we are led by the Spirit. Jews, Gentiles, Protestants, Catholics, black, white, rich, poor, genius, average, as long as we are filled with the Spirit, as long as we follow the standards and principles of God's Kingdom, as long as we forsake the deeds of the flesh, we are all one in Christ and therefore are in God's image, and will consequently all inherit the Kingdom of Heaven.

PERSONAL APPLICATION
CHANGE IS NOT INEVITABLE

We go through changes our entire lives and many times it is both easy and desirable. I'm talking about the different stages of human development

1. Pre-natal

2. Infancy and babyhood

3. Early childhood

4. Late childhood

5. Adolescence

6. Early adulthood

7. Old age

For everyone who develops normally, these stages come naturally. Most of us take great pleasure moving from one stage to the other, perhaps with one notable exception (you guess which one). If throughout our existence we go through changes, why then is change so difficult for most of us to accept? Even with these stages of development, while they come natural physically, it's not always so easy to adjust mentally.

If an adolescent does not change (i.e. develop) to the next stage, they will miss out on all of the perks of adulthood. Similarly, we cannot enjoy the benefits of the Kingdom unless we are prepared to change. As long as the adolescent acts the same way and does the same things, it does not matter how much their physical bodies develop, because their minds are the same, they are in effect still adolescents. We will not be able to be a part of God's family as long as we do everything the same as we did before.

Changing is difficult, but that's okay. As long as we keep working at it, with the help of the Holy Spirit, we will overcome our challenges. We must therefore not accept spiritual mediocrity. I've heard many persons who held senior positions professionally claim to be a "spiritual person." I used to say it too. I didn't use those exact words, but the meaning was the same. My exact words were something like this: "I may not be everything God wants me to be, but God knows my heart." However, every time those words came out of my mouth, I saw them for what they were…excuses. I was afraid to take the next step. Most of the times, I was afraid because I tried too many times and failed. But this is what growing pains are.

No one moves from one stage of development to the other without growing pains. Every step has its challenges and setbacks. Unfortunately, Christians often overlook this and get stuck. And most of the times, we get stuck because we mess up and get discouraged. God wants us to become mature in Him. He wants us to keep growing. He wants us to persist. From science, we learn that anything that is not growing, is decaying. This is also true spiritually. We must continue to grow, or else we are like 'dead men walking'.

Jesus commands us to CHANGE. It is time for God's children to advance to the next level of our spiritual development. What's your next level? What changes do you need to make?

Section 2

Kingdom Life

Jesus came to give us life; life more abundantly.

John 10:10 (KJV) The thief cometh not, but for to steal, and to kill, and to destroy: <u>*I am come that they might have life, and that they might have it more*</u> <u>*abundantly*</u>.

Having life means that we have to live. Teaching us how to live was one of the central purposes of Jesus.

John 8:12 (KJV) Then spake Jesus again unto them, saying, I am the light of the world: he that followeth me shall not walk in darkness, but shall have the light of life.

To be WITH Jesus, we must learn to be LIKE Jesus!

In this section, we explore the life that Jesus taught us to live. We also learn how God empowers us to live like Jesus.

.

Chapter 4

Kingdom Citizens
(Children of God)

John 1:12-13 (KJV) ¹²*But as many as received him, to them gave he power to become the sons of God, even to them that believe on his name:* ¹³*Which were born, not of blood, nor of the will of the flesh, nor of the will of man, but of God.*

There are several avenues whereby citizenship is granted. Typically, citizenship is automatically granted to children who are born in the country of their parents. In many countries, a child is able to qualify for citizenship in the country of their parents, regardless of their actual place of birth. Citizenship can also be obtained by foreigners through naturalization. Obviously, the process will differ for each country, but these are some of the more common ways that citizenship is passed to individuals. John, in his gospel, summarized these into three broad categories: blood, the will of the flesh, and the will of man.

Not of Blood

Because citizenship (or sonship with God) into the Kingdom of God cannot be obtained by physical birth, John, a Jew himself, was making a very personal and profound statement to his Jewish brothers and sisters. He was deliberately and directly refuting the concept that salvation was exclusively for the Jews, or that the Jews as a people have a special right or access to God that the rest of us non-Jews do not have. **Kingdom citizenship is not bestowed from generational lineage. Not of blood!**

In many countries around the world, illegal immigration is a major problem. Illegal immigrants tend to consume a lot of the limited resources of the host country. This is problematic because host countries rightly see their resources as belonging to themselves and persons who reside legally. Resources are needed for food, shelter, education, health care, environment, security, infrastructure, etc., and in all cases, these resources are limited. Add to this, instances where the illegal immigrant populations may grow at a faster rate than natural-born citizens, the chances for major civil dispute escalates. Because of these challenges, illegal immigrants are frowned upon in many otherwise civilized nations.

One of the greatest nations in the world today, at least in terms of economic power, the United States of America, struggles with this and has for a long time. In 2016, Mr. Donald Trump, had as his main presidential campaign platform, that he would stop illegal immigration. He proposed to build a wall to keep illegal immigrants out of the United States. His American opponents felt that his approach to dealing with the issue disregarded the positive contributions many migrants made to building and making America strong. This disagreement has gone on for many years, with no end in sight.

In my country, The Bahamas, we too have a similar challenge with the Haitian illegal migrants. Many Bahamians, including many Christians, are frustrated about the illegal immigration situation here. Even though over the years, Bahamians have become more tolerant, still, there are too many of us who, through our words, disparage our Haitian brothers and sisters, who are only seeking a better life for themselves and their families.

The same problem exists in other countries around the world. Even when there have been high profile, public, justifiable reasons people have fled their country, many neighbouring countries either block access or limit the number of persons they allow on a humanitarian basis to enter their country legally. A good example of this is the mixed response to the Syrian refugee crisis since the war in 2011. While many neighbouring countries have assisted greatly with this crisis, several prominent countries have not.

We can glean from certain Bible passages that they also faced similar challenges back then. For example, the Jews saw people like the Samaritans very negatively. There is a popular phrase echoed in the scriptures that the Jews have no dealings with the Samaritans. When Jesus went through Samaria, at Jacob's well, he asked a Samaritan woman for something to drink. Her snappy response to Him, which reverberates today, was to ask Him why He was asking her for water since it was common knowledge that the Jews despised the Samaritans, as evidenced by their refusal to deal with them.

In another example, Jesus, although He clearly did not support such a position, used this posturing to make a point when the Syrophoenician Woman asked Him to deliver her daughter from the demons that afflicted her. Jesus' answer was that He was not sent but "to the lost sheep of the house of Israel" and that it is "not meet to take the children's bread, and to cast it to dogs." These statements alienated her and must have hurt her deeply because all she wanted was help and relief for her daughter's possession. But she persisted. Later, He concluded that her faith was great, then He healed her daughter. Jesus put her through that experience to test her faith much the same way God tested the faith of Abraham, asking him to sacrifice his son Isaac. I strongly believe that neither tests were meant to establish a hermeneutical position based solely on the actual tests, but of the faith being tested. No more did Jesus come only for the house of Israel than God intended people to sacrifice their children to Him.

The point here is that the negative side of citizenship is unwanted immigration, and thanks be to God, Kingdom citizenship does not have this problem because Kingdom citizenship is not passed down by birth. Anyone can become a citizen. Equally important, everyone can be a citizen. <u>No matter how full, there is room for more in God's Kingdom.</u> You will not be turned away. You will not be stopped at any inspection points. You will not be ill-treated within the Kingdom. There are no wall or Immigration or Border Patrol inspectors whose job is to keep you out. Your application for citizenship will be processed immediately and will not be rejected!

Nor of the will of the flesh

John also said that citizenship is not determined by the will of the flesh. In some nations, persons gain citizenship by marriage. Most laws in developed countries allow citizenship to be passed on to a spouse after going through certain hurdles. In The Bahamas, a non-Bahamian having been married to a Bahamian may qualify for citizenship after seven years of marriage, among other qualifying criteria. Other countries similarly have their own requirements, which allow the transference of citizenship. However, there are issues with this as persons have effectively sold citizenship to others, which is illegal in most countries. Not so in the Kingdom of God because, as John said, citizenship cannot be passed through the flesh.

Nor of the will of man

The day we stood before the Magistrate and affirmed our desire to become guardians of A'Mya, she became a part of our household. Automatically, we were granted certain rights and responsibilities over her life. We immediately took on a legal responsibility to provide for her and to protect her. We also instantly received power to make decisions for her. Prior to that court ruling, we had no such rights or responsibilities.

Under the Mosaic Laws, along with other requirements, it was necessary for Jewish converts to be circumcised. This practise continued even after Jesus' resurrection. In Acts 15, a major dispute erupted when the Gentile Christian movement started to grow. Certain Jews demanded that they become circumcised else, so they were told, they could not be saved (Acts 15:1). Because of this, Paul and Barnabas were sent back to Jerusalem to discuss this matter with the Apostles, to get direction and clarity. After a long debate, it was agreed that circumcision was not needed.

John made it clear that no other formalities of governments, be they legislative or judicial, can bestow Kingdom citizenship ("nor by the will of man"). You cannot obtain citizenship by naturalization, by making investments, or any other way. It must be by the will of God. John was making a definitive yet scorching statement to his Jewish brothers that Israel is not singularly the chosen people of God, nor was there any way to become a part of God's Kingdom except by believing in Jesus.

Gentiles

Earlier in This Book, we pointed out that when he penned the words in chapter 1, John was attempting to show his Jewish brothers and sisters that Jesus came to broadened the hypothetical borders of the chosen nation to include more than just Jews. There are many references in the old testament that prove that God had a plan to invite all Gentiles into His Kingdom.

Jonah, a Hebrew prophet, was sent to preach to Nineveh. Nineveh was a Gentile nation, the capital of the Assyrian Empire, yet God showed His mercy toward them in that He sent Jonah to warn them about their impending destruction in 40 days. When they repented, God was merciful to them and spared them. Consider how important the people of Nineveh were to God. Ponder the things that He caused Jonah to suffer because he did not want to go to that Gentile nation. While Jonah may have devalued their lives, God placed tremendous value on the people of

Nineveh. Don't you think this is an extraordinary length for God to go through for a people that He does not care deeply about, or that He does not consider to be His own? It is clear to me that His love extended beyond Israel even then.

Isaiah, the Prophet, was more prolific, having addressed this subject matter multiple times. One of his most transparent references is found in the following text:

Isaiah 56:3-8 (KJV) ³***Neither let the son of the stranger, that hath joined himself to the Lord, speak, saying, The Lord hath utterly separated me from his people****: neither let the eunuch say, Behold, I am a dry tree. ⁴For thus saith the Lord unto the eunuchs that keep my sabbaths, and choose the things that please me, and take hold of my covenant;* ⁵***Even unto them will I give in mine house and within my walls a place and a name better than of sons and of daughters****: I will give them an everlasting name, that shall not be cut off. ⁶Also the sons of the stranger, that join themselves to the Lord, to serve him, and to love the name of the Lord, to be his servants, every one that keepeth the sabbath from polluting it, and taketh hold of my covenant; ⁷Even them will I bring to my holy mountain, and make them joyful in my house of prayer: their burnt offerings and their sacrifices shall be accepted upon mine altar;* ***for mine house shall be called an house of prayer <u>for all people</u>****. ⁸The Lord God, which gathereth the outcasts of Israel saith,* ***Yet will I gather others to him, beside those that are gathered unto him****.*

Of course, we all know that God called Paul to preach to the Gentiles and to bring salvation to them (see Acts 22:21). The Gentiles were always a part of God's plan to be His children. John understood this when he said that the right to become a child of God is not of blood (like the Jewish lineage), nor of the will of the flesh (by some fleshly ritual), nor of the will of man (by some legislative or judicial framework on the transfer of citizenship), but of God.

<u>But of God</u>

While there may be many ways to become a citizen of earthly nations, there is only one way to become a citizen of the Kingdom of God. We have to become a child of God. Frankly, I do not like using the word citizen when it comes to the Kingdom because it connotes similarity with worldly citizenship. This is not quite what God envisioned for His Kingdom. His concept is more closely aligned with family (Father/Son/Daughter) than a nation (citizens). He wants us to be His children, not His citizens. Here are some scriptures that speak to this:

*John 1:12 (KJV) But as many as received him, to them gave he **power to become the sons of God**, even to them that believe on his name:*

*Philippians 2:14-15 (KJV) ¹⁴Do all things without murmurings and disputings: ¹⁵That ye may be blameless and harmless, **the sons of God**, without rebuke, in the midst of a crooked and perverse nation, among whom ye shine as lights in the world;*

*Romans 8:14-15 (KJV) ¹⁴For as many as are led by the Spirit of God, **they are the sons of God**. ¹⁵ For ye have not received the spirit of bondage again to fear; but ye have received the Spirit of adoption, whereby we cry, Abba, Father.*

*Ephesians 2:19 (KJV) Now therefore ye are no more strangers and foreigners, but fellowcitizens with the saints, **and of the household of God**;*

Each of these scriptures speaks about a personal relationship with God, one closer than a mere citizen to a King. They speak about family, about sons and daughters of God. Even the Ephesians text, which is directly addressing citizenship, still adds a more intimate and familial relationship "of the household of God." Notice also that some of these scriptures make a connection between the Holy Spirit and sonship with God. We will explore this association more in chapter 6 - Kingdom Guide (Holy Spirit).

We become "citizens" by becoming children of God. John 1:12 shows that we become children of God by believing in Jesus and receiving Him into our hearts. Believing on Him means believing that He is the Christ, the firstborn son of God, and the Saviour of the world. Receiving Him in our hearts means living in accordance with His commandments and following His example. In the gospel, John said that Jesus gave us power to become sons of God. This power is extended to everyone.

*Galatians 4:1-7 (KJV) Now I say, That the heir, as long as he is a child, differeth nothing from a servant, though he be lord of all; ² But is under tutors and governors until the time appointed of the father. ³ Even so we, when we were children, were in bondage under the elements of the world: ⁴ But when the fulness of the time was come, God sent forth his Son, made of a woman, made under the law, ⁵ **To redeem them that were under the law, that we might receive the adoption of sons**. ⁶ And because ye are sons, God hath sent forth the Spirit of his Son into your hearts, crying, Abba, Father. ⁷ **Wherefore thou art no more a servant, but a son; and if a son, then an heir of God through Christ.***

This confirms the notion that our relationship with God is more of a father/child than that of a ruler/subject or king/citizen. This is also a really educational scripture about the relationship between God vis-à-vis the Jews and Gentiles. As we indicated, Paul was called by Christ to preach to the Gentiles. Prior to this, the Gentiles were treated as outsiders from Israel, and even if they became a part of Israel, they had inferior rights under the Laws. In this letter to the Galatians, Paul put Jews and Gentiles on equal footing when it came to sonship. In verse 5, he said that God sent Jesus into the world "to redeem them that were under the law that we might receive the adoption of sons." The Jews (those under the law) must make the same path to God as the Gentiles. They, too, have to be adopted, and through that adoption, we all become sons (and daughters) of God.

God is truly no respecter of persons. Neither is He a respecter of nations. Here's what Peter said after he finally accepted that God also called Gentiles to be His people:

Acts 10:34-35 (KJV) [34] *Then Peter opened his mouth, and said, Of a truth I perceive that **God is no respecter of persons:*** [35] ***But in every nation he that feareth him, and worketh righteousness, is accepted with him.***

Becoming a child of God makes God our Father. This is the most amazing thing in the whole Bible. Our Father happens to be:

- The creator of the whole world

- The giver of life

- Omnipotent – all-powerful

- Omniscient – all-knowing

- Omnipresent – all present

- Sovereign – everything is subject to Him

These are the attributes of our Father. They are not ours. Although we are His children, they are not ours to command. But God loves us. Jesus promised His disciples that anything that they ask in His name, He would pray to the Father, and the Father will give it. This promise carries over to those of us who, through Jesus and the Holy Spirit, become sons of God. The key provision, however, is that we must ask in Jesus' name. This means that the things we ask for are subject to the will of Jesus. James said that we ask and do not receive because we ask amiss.

James 4:2-3 (KJV) ²Ye lust, and have not: ye kill, and desire to have, and cannot obtain: ye fight and war, yet ye have not, because ye ask not. ³Ye ask, and receive not, because ye ask amiss, that ye may consume it upon your lusts.

It turns out that the promise that our Father will give us what we ask is not open-ended. We can't ask for any and everything we want. Even Jesus couldn't, as we learned when Jesus asked for the cup to be taken away (the cup being the burden he would have to bear in his crucifixion at the hands of His accusers). But that wasn't the first time that we learned that Jesus couldn't just ask for anything He wanted. Jesus Himself confirmed this when He responded to the devil's temptation. In Matthew 4:7, Jesus told the devil that He would not test the power of God just to confirm His status as the Son of God because the Bible says that we must not test (or tempt) God. The history of this response went back to the day the Hebrews tested God because they wanted confirmation that He was with them (see Exodus 17). Jesus is saying to us all today that we must not test God with frivolity, personal goals or lusts, or anything else for that matter.

God operates with impunity. He has the final word on everything, and that final word may be NO. We should not assume no is the answer. We should ask, just like Jesus encouraged us to ask, and we should persist in our asking even while acknowledging that if the final answer is no, we are prepared to gladly accept God's will and move on. The key thing to remember is that just as Jesus is the Son of God, so are we, and as sons, we have the ultimate God in our Father who can do anything. But He is not to be trifled with.

We also see in verse 3 of the above scripture the whole outside looking inward problem again. When we look from the outside in to see how we can obtain things that we are lusting after for our own benefits, God is under no obligation to provide it to us. Why don't we start asking and seeking things that will benefit others, and watch God give us the desires of our hearts, which incidentally will be to benefit others.

Renunciation

Just as a citizen of any country can renounce their citizenship, so can a child of God separate themselves from God. Paul explained this to the Corinthians in this manner:

1 Corinthians 6:9-10 (KJV) *⁹**Know ye not that the unrighteous shall not inherit the kingdom of God?***Be not deceived: neither fornicators, nor idolaters, nor adulterers, nor effeminate, nor abusers of themselves with mankind, ¹⁰Nor thieves, nor covetous, nor drunkards, nor revilers, nor extortioners, shall inherit the kingdom of God.*

Renunciation is normally a voluntary legal act that a citizen must undertake to relinquish their citizenship. Once a person becomes a citizen in a country, they typically retain that status until they renounce their citizenship. It's much the same in the Kingdom with respect to our status as children of God. However, our acts of renunciation from the Kingdom are less formal and, therefore, much more subtle, and because it's subtle, we can very easily lose our sonship with God. As Paul explained above, **we lose our rights to the Kingdom by being unrighteous.** That's why Jesus warned us to seek the Kingdom of God "and His righteousness" in Matthew 6:33.

Focus, Refocus

Christ's message about the Kingdom was meant to refocus Israel and everyone else who would believe in Jesus and on God's actual promise of a Kingdom, rather than Israel's narrow-minded hopes of becoming a world superpower. Deuteronomy 15:6 says, "thou shalt reign over many nations, but they shall not reign over thee." Contrary to this, Israel had been subject to many years of captivity under multiple regimes, including the Egyptians, Greeks, Persians, and others. But the Jews thought that the scriptures prophesied that God would eventually raise a King <u>on earth</u> and would, through that King, make them once and ever thereafter the superpower of this world. Even the disciples bought into this. They asked Jesus in Acts 1:6, "Lord, wilt thou at this time restore again the kingdom to Israel."

They asked this question because Jesus had died and was risen. His power was indisputable. He had power over death. But instead, He told them that He would leave them. They must have been disappointed. Do you remember when they argued about who would be greatest in His Kingdom? They expected Jesus to become the

King, and they were lining up for high positions in the Kingdom. They must have been very disappointed that Jesus was leaving them without establishing His kingdom in Israel. He did not make them a world superpower as they had been taught, and as they expected. Perhaps it was disappointing to them, but for the rest of us, it meant hope. Hope that we could be a part of the Kingdom of God. Otherwise, we would have no rights to the Kingdom, and we would be outsiders to God–those of us who are not Jews, that is. Jesus' combined message to Israel was that it had to change its behaviour and its focus to the true message and intent of God. That message was about righteousness.

The authors of the new testament letters also understood the principles of the Kingdom, though they rarely quoted the word Kingdom. It's because the Kingdom of God is about more than what we conceptualize in a kingdom based on our worldly knowledge of kingdoms. It's also because God did not intend us to use the concept of the kingdom to separate His people from other people (like governments separate their people), but to help us understand His purpose for our daily living.

Romans 14:17 (KJV) For the kingdom of God is not meat and drink; but righteousness, and peace, and joy in the Holy Ghost.

Paul put it succinctly that the Kingdom is not about meat and drink, but about righteousness, peace, and joy in the Holy Spirit. Notice that there is no reference, either directly or otherwise, to governments, laws, even citizenship. Also, notice that the reference to the Holy Ghost keeps popping up in conjunction with the kingdom. The relationship between the Holy Spirit and the Kingdom of God are both inseparable and substantial, so much that we dedicated a full chapter of This Book to illuminate it. For now, we need to understand that this is Kingdom "citizenship." Becoming a child of God (as defined previously) with the aid of the Holy Spirit is the only way to gain access to the Kingdom.

*Romans 8:13-16 (KJV) [13]For if ye live after the flesh, ye shall die: but if ye **through the Spirit** do mortify the deeds of the body, ye shall live. [14]**For as many as are led by the Spirit of God, they are the sons of God.** [15]For ye have not received the spirit of bondage again to fear; **but ye have received the Spirit of adoption, whereby we cry, Abba, Father.** [16]**The Spirit itself beareth witness with our spirit, that we are the children of God***

If verse 14 is indeed accurate (and it is), that those of us who are led by the Spirit of God are the sons of God, then by extension of this thought, if we are not led by the Spirit of God, our sonship is questionable at best. Truly, there is no sonship with God without being filled by His Holy Spirit.

PERSONAL APPLICATION
SOMETIMES THE ANSWER IS NO

Good parents try to be impartial toward their children. Even if they actually favour one child above the others, good parents try not to let that negatively affect the other children. Sometimes good parents have to say no to a child for no other reason than the fact that they simply don't have sufficient resources to give to everyone. On the other hand, sometimes good parents have to spend more time with certain children who need it than others who don't. Sometimes they have to be harder on one child than others. This discourse shows that parents have to consider their children from two different perspectives–as an individual child, and as part of the family.

As children of God, it is important that we recognize that God also deals with us as part of the Kingdom family, and as individuals within the Kingdom. Some of us seem to be more favoured than others, that is, more blessed. Some of us definitely have a harder life than others. This dynamic is complicated when we are inundated with a homogenous gospel that tells us that we are the same when it comes to God's blessings. We are often told that the blessings of God are for everyone, but this kind of gospel message is crippling the lives of many persons who do not understand that sometimes God in His wisdom allows some of us to go through hardship, while He delivers others. This is because God knows everything and He has plans that we cannot comprehend. Unlike some, I do not believe Jesus, while on earth, was wealthy; and regardless of His finances, though He was God in human form, Jesus suffered more than most of us could ever imagine. His life was not all a bed of deliciousness. But God allowed Him to suffer because He had a plan that needed to be fulfilled. Jesus asked God to take the cup (of suffering) away from Him. God said NO!

The children of Israel suffered under the oppression of the Egyptians for 400 years. That's a long time. Over those years, a lot of people were born into bondage and died because of the bondage. Year after year, they suffered, cried out to God, and died having not been delivered. Until one day, Moses was chosen to lead them to freedom.

As a black person, our ethnicity has suffered many years of oppression. Even in a predominantly black country, The Bahamas has a history of slavery and its ghastly effects. Many of our ancestors were born and died in it. But today, we enjoy freedom in a democratic country, led by the people we choose. Today they are black. For our ancestors, God said no, but He used them to effect the changes needed to tell us YES.

There is hope for those of us who are told no, who are lacking compared to others. Consider this popular scripture in 1 Corinthians 12:20-27

20But now are they many members (INDIVIDUALS), yet but one body (KINGDOM). 21And the eye cannot say unto the hand, I have no need of thee: nor again the head to the feet, I have no need of you. 22Nay, much more those members of the body, which seem to be more feeble, are necessary: 23And those members of the body, which we think to be less honourable, upon these we bestow more abundant honour; and our uncomely parts have more abundant comeliness. 24For our comely parts have no need: but God hath tempered the body together, having given more abundant honour to that part which lacked. 25That there should be no schism in the body; but that the members should have the same care one for another. 26And whether one member suffer, all the members suffer with it; or one member be honoured, all the members rejoice with it. 27Now ye are the body of Christ, and members in particular.

Those of us who are told NO have the assurance that God sees our deficiencies. But not only that, He places more honour on us for what we have to endure, than those who have less struggles. Paul also said of such people that this world is not worthy of them–implying that the time of their many blessings is yet to come. Hebrews 11:36-40

36And others had trial of cruel mockings and scourgings, yea, moreover of bonds and imprisonment: 37They were stoned, they were sawn asunder, were tempted, were slain with the sword: they wandered about in sheepskins and goatskins; being destitute, afflicted, tormented; 38(Of whom the world was not worthy:) they wandered in deserts, and in mountains, and in dens and caves of the earth. 39And these all, having obtained a good report through faith, received not the promise: 40God having provided some better thing for us, that they without us should not be made perfect.

We may not be told yes too many times in this life; in fact, there are many times we have to say no to this world; but our blessings are accruing to our benefit in God's Kingdom, and that's where it really matters.

Patrick James McFall

Chapter 5

Kingdom Come
(New Commandments)

With the obvious exceptions of His death and resurrection, ushering in the Kingdom of God was perhaps the most important objective that Jesus came on earth to achieve. There are 162 references to Kingdom in the new testament. This alone sheds some light on the significance of the Kingdom, but it barely scratches the surface in revealing its magnitude. Jesus preached about the Kingdom of God from the onset of His ministry. The first reference to the Kingdom of Heaven is found in Matthew, chapter 4.

Matthew 4:17 (KJV) From that time Jesus began to preach, and to say, Repent: for the kingdom of Heaven is at hand.

The fact that Matthew says "from that time" indicates a constant and consistent message throughout Jesus' life and ministry preaching about repentance and the coming of God's Kingdom. Through His short life and ministry, Jesus taught many things about the Kingdom. Wikipedia referenced 37 direct messages about the Kingdom. However, these are only in the parables. Frankly, and more importantly, every message Jesus gave had relevance to the Kingdom, even when He didn't use the word Kingdom specifically. All of His teachings collectively were intended to prepare Israel, and the rest of us, for life in the Kingdom...His Kingdom...God's Kingdom.

When will His Kingdom come?

The Kingdom of God is definitely a big deal, and there are a lot of materials about the Kingdom available today. Many authors have set out to reveal the mysteries of the Kingdom. Some authors have multiple books about the Kingdom, writing from as many angles as imaginable. There remains, however, some confusion out there as some of the teachings about the Kingdom appear in opposition to each other. Some teach that the Kingdom is about life with God after we die; that we will inherit the new earth prophesied in Revelation. Others teach that it is about life here and now, and that we must reclaim the earth on God's behalf. Some teach that as Kingdom citizens, we are to be kings and to exercise influence over the worldly systems. They teach that as Kingdom citizens, we have power on earth and that the manifestation of that power is evidence of the Kingdom. Others teach that we are to be servants, as Jesus taught His disciples when asked: "who is the greatest in the kingdom of heaven." In their view, the manifestation of the Kingdom is seen in service to God and man. Such confusion is completely understandable. For years, I was confused about these and other questions because there are different scriptures that seem to support both. Take, for example, the Parable of the Tares. In His interpretation of the parable, Jesus said this:

> *Matthew 13:37-38 (KJV)* *37He answered and said unto them, He that soweth the good seed is the Son of man;* *38**The field is the world; the good seed are the children of the kingdom**; but the tares are the children of the wicked one;*

The bold text seems to indirectly connect the world and the children of the Kingdom. One can easily infer that some element of the Kingdom pertains to life on earth. Because of this, there are some people who teach that the Kingdom exists concurrently with the world today, and hence, Believers have dual citizenship, one in their earthly country, and the other in the Kingdom of God. They envision an actual spiritual kingdom existing parallel to our natural lives, here on earth. In this kingdom, some believe that there is currency (faith), laws (the Bible), and territories to conquer on God's behalf.

Conversely, there are others who see scriptures that explicitly indicate that the Kingdom of God will be inherited **after death**. Read the parable of the ten talents in Matthew 25. At the conclusion of the parable, Jesus gave this stunning recap that seems to leave no doubt that the kingdom is about the future.

> *Matthew 25:31-34 (KJV)* *31When the Son of man shall come in his glory, and all the holy angels with him, **then shall he sit upon the throne of his glory:*** *32And before him shall be gathered all nations: and he shall separate them one from another, as a shepherd divideth his sheep from the goats:* *33And he shall set the sheep on his right hand, but the goats on the left.* *34Then shall the King say unto them on*

*his right hand, Come, ye blessed of my Father, **inherit the kingdom prepared for you from the foundation of the world**:*

Here's what Peter said about this subject:

*2 Peter 3:13 (KJV) Nevertheless **we, according to his promise, look for new heavens and a new earth**, wherein dwelleth righteousness.*

Clearer reference that the Kingdom is about the future could not have been made than in these scriptures. Jesus had to die, and He has to return before He sits on His throne. We, too, have to die (more specifically, be changed) to inherit the Kingdom. As the above scripture from Matthew explains, ultimately, **we can only inherit the Kingdom after the judgment**. But today, we must follow the Holy Spirit on this earthly journey, just as the children of Israel followed Joshua before ultimately taking possession of their promised land. We have to be prepared before we can enter, and that preparation has already started. This preparation is what Jesus was referring to in the Parable of the Tares.

Even after they crossed over Jordan, the Hebrews did not immediately possess the land. They had to systematically defeat the enemies who were in the land before they could possess it. One story in Joshua confirmed that victory was not assured. The children of Israel were defeated when they went up against the Canaanites at Ai because Achan sinned against God. This reveals to us that we are living in a transitory place where we are preparing to inherit the Kingdom, but where we also can be disqualified if we sin against God. Paul put it this way when speaking about Abraham, Sarah, and the other forerunners in Israel:

*Hebrews 11:13-16 (KJV) [13] These all died in faith, **not** having received the promises, but having seen them afar off, and were persuaded of them, and embraced them, and **confessed that they were strangers and pilgrims on the earth**. [14] For they that say such things declare plainly that they seek a country. [15] And truly, if they had been mindful of that country from whence they came out, they might have had opportunity to have returned. [16] **But now they desire a better country, that is, an heavenly**: wherefore God is not ashamed to be called their God: **for he hath prepared for them a city**.*

This dichotomy about the timing of the coming of God's kingdom reveals one of the major threats Christians face. It's an age-old challenge that even the early church had to deal with. In fact, it first reared its nasty head the day Satan deceived Eve. It is that the search for truth is very difficult, and more so now that we live in the age of information, whereby it is easy to disburse untruths to the world. Apostle Peter alluded to this issue in his second epistle:

*2 Peter 2:1-3 (KJV) ¹But there were false prophets also among the people, even as **there shall be false teachers among you**, who privily shall bring in damnable heresies, even denying the Lord that bought them, and bring upon themselves swift destruction. ²And many shall follow their pernicious ways; **by reason of whom the way of truth shall be evil spoken of**. ³And through covetousness shall they **with feigned words make merchandise of you**: whose judgment now of a long time lingereth not, and their damnation slumbereth not.*

Christians must be careful about who they follow, and this includes whose doctrine they follow. Sometimes we follow persons who we believe should be knowledgeable and trustworthy because of their position and status. They may occupy positions of trust, like a school teacher, pastor, politician, friend, etc. However, some of them are teaching errors and leading us down the wrong path, abusing us to advance themselves. That's what Peter was saying then, and it's still happening today.

Paul, too, wrote about this challenge with error teachings.

*1 Timothy 6:3-6 (KJV) ³If any man teach otherwise, and consent not to wholesome words, even the words of our Lord Jesus Christ, and to the doctrine which is according to godliness; ⁴He is proud, knowing nothing, but doting about questions and strifes of words, whereof cometh envy, strife, railings, evil surmisings, ⁵Perverse disputings of men of corrupt minds, and **destitute of the truth, supposing that gain is godliness: from such withdraw thyself**. ⁶But godliness with contentment is great gain.*

This is why I undertook to write This Book; to help Believers navigate the TRUTH regarding the Kingdom of God. This Book is intended to share the teachings of Jesus about His Kingdom because there are many expectations that He has of us that He disclosed in His messages, a lot of which have been moderated, thereby diminishing their impact on our lives. A lot of His lessons have become substituted by their antithesis, doctrines about prosperity, and its less abrasive yet nonetheless selfish brother, success, which both have the same foundation as "gain is godliness." Many things that are taught about the Kingdom flows from this vantage point of personal achievements being the evidence of godliness.

We are too often taught that Kingdom citizens should be the head and not the tail, and we interpret this to mean that Christians should be at the top of every organization, group, or anything else in this life. Contrary to the scriptures, many popular religious leaders teach this as evidence of right standing with God. As we can see, Paul told Timothy that these are persons that we should avoid when he said: "from such withdraw thyself."

Kingdom Come, Will be Done

In the Lord's prayer, Jesus taught His disciples to pray and included the words "Thy Kingdom come. Thy will be done in earth, as it is in Heaven." Jesus was instructing them to pray that something that exists in Heaven be duplicated on earth. He was signaling that change was needed on earth. What exactly did He mean? Can God's kingdom literally come on earth as it is in Heaven?

We know that Jesus said that His Kingdom is not of this world. He made this abundantly clear in John 18:36. If His kingdom is not of this world, then it is unlikely that He was telling us to pray that His kingdom would come in this world. No, He didn't teach us to pray that God's physical kingdom come on earth as it is in Heaven. He actually taught us to pray that God's Kingdom would come...PERIOD! It is "God's will" that He taught should be done on earth as it is in Heaven; that's what He taught us to pray! **He wants God's will to be done on earth as it is in Heaven.** However, this point may very well be a distinction without a difference because I believe both statements virtually meant the same.

"Thy will be done!" Who do you think He meant to do God's will? It's doubtful He was referring to anyone who currently resides in Heaven since everyone living there is completely committed to His will. **'Thy kingdom come' is an invitation for God's system of rulership, yes, His Kingdom to be established.** God's Kingdom operates under God's will since He is the God of this Kingdom. We established earlier that God is inward-out looking. We also established His character—mercy, gracious, longsuffering, etc. (from Exodus 34:6-7). These are the things that Jesus wants to be established on earth. This is the Kingdom that He wants to come. That's why He said that the Kingdom is within us (Luke 17:20-21).

When Satan was in Heaven, he tried to establish a different set of standards than that laid out by God. He looked outward-in. He wanted glory, power, and exultation. When he realized that God wasn't about to let that happened (because pride, arrogance, and self-promotion are unacceptable to God), instead of accepting God's sovereignty, he decided to challenge God's will and recruited other angels to support his perverted vision for Heaven. God rejected this way, rejected Lucifer, and threw him out of Heaven because he did not yield to God's will. This is why only those of us who choose to follow God's will, will be accepted in Heaven. Asking for His Kingdom to come is akin to asking for His will to be done. Asking for His will to be done, is akin to asking for us to follow God's way of life.

What is God's will? What is God's way of life? The best way to know God's will and His way of life is to understand His commandments.

Kingdom Lifestyle

When Jesus started preaching the Sermon on the Mount, He effectively started to teach about His Kingdom lifestyle. The Jews were waiting on a King to be established within Israel, one who would deliver them from the Roman empire and make the kingdom of Israel the victor and leader among the nations of the world. When He started talking about the Kingdom coming soon, their ears were perked up. This is what they were all waiting for and praying for. Not so fast, though! Jesus had a very different opinion about His Kingdom. His message was almost the opposite from what the Jewish scholars (Pharisees, Sadducees, and lawyers) taught. Jesus came preaching about humility, love, mercy, gentleness, fairness, and sacrifice. These were the principles of the Kingdom as foretold in the old testament. We have already seen how these align with the image of God, as defined by God Himself.

Jesus taught that the pursuit of wealth is to take a back seat to the pursuit of God. He taught that the greatest person is the one who served, rather than the one being served, just as He is Master of us all, yet He came serving (John 13:1-17). So, His message was somewhat in contrast to what the scribes and Pharisees believed and taught. And, while this message is preached on pulpits around the world, it is interwoven with messages about prosperity, self-indulgence (personal wealth and success) and selfishness (giving to others as a means to get more for ourselves).

In the Sermon on the Mount, Jesus established His own commandments for us to live by. Commandments, which, if followed, would bring us back to God's image. In Matthew 5:17, Jesus said He came to fulfill the law and the prophets; He perfected their message and commandments with His own. Further support that these are His commandments can be seen in the scripture below, where Jesus referred to "these least commandments" and linked them to the Kingdom of Heaven three times.

Matthew 5:19-20 (KJV) *¹⁹Whosoever therefore shall break **one of these least commandments**, and shall teach men so, he shall be called the least in the **kingdom of heaven**: but whosoever shall do and teach them, the same shall be called great in the **kingdom of heaven**. ²⁰For I say unto you, That except your righteousness shall exceed the righteousness of the scribes and Pharisees, ye shall in no case enter into the **kingdom of heaven**.*

Many of us may mistakenly assume verse 19 was referring to the Mosaic Laws, but He was talking about His Kingdom commandments instead. If He were speaking about the Laws, then adherence to the Laws would have resulted in righteousness. That's why He referred to righteousness in verse 20. He wanted us to know that following the Laws could not result in righteousness. The religious leaders sought to obtain righteousness by the law, and Jesus said that this is not the way. Paul confirmed this in Galatians 2:21 when he said: "I do not frustrate the grace of God: for if righteousness come by the law, then Christ is dead in vain."

Let's put these two thoughts together now and see the conclusion of the matter. If righteousness comes by keeping "these least commandments" (according to Jesus), and if righteousness does not come by the law (according to Jesus and Paul), then the commandments to which Jesus was referring must be different from the laws, otherwise, these scriptures contradict each other. Only through Jesus and His righteousness, that is, through following His commandments, can we enter into the Kingdom of Heaven.

Since His people did not understand His Kingdom commandments yet, Jesus used the entire message on the Kingdom Sermon on the Mount to both establish His Kingdom commandments and rebuff certain Laws of the kingdom of Israel. It's true that Jesus said that He did not come to destroy the Laws or the prophets. He said He came to fulfill them (Matthew 5:17). Therefore, while He did not come to destroy them, He produced some sort of change in them, which He described as fulfilling them. Before Jesus, the Laws were incomplete. Jesus came to complete them. They were previously deficient. Jesus brought clarity to their deficiencies and thereby corrected them. Consider the many times during the Kingdom Sermon that Jesus refuted the Laws of Moses and in place established new "laws" or commandments for us to follow. Six times between verse 21 and verse 48 of Matthew 5, did Jesus show

how the Laws of Moses were lacking. Six times He said some version of "Ye have heard that it was said of them of old time...**But I say unto you**." These bolded words certainly sound an awful lot like commandments.

To better understand the Kingdom lifestyle that Jesus espoused, let's delve deeper into the Kingdom Sermon on the Mount–the first recorded and greatest message about the Kingdom of God.

Kingdom Commandments, not Beatitudes!

Some of the Kingdom Sermon are commonly referred to as the Beatitudes, but more appropriately, they are part of Jesus' **Kingdom Commandments**. They are commandments because that's what Jesus called them. They're about the Kingdom because that's what Jesus went about preaching throughout His ministry. By calling them beatitudes, we have effectively watered them down; and I'm not speaking about the Jews either. We as Christians water these Kingdom commandments down.

Calling them beatitudes treats them like suggestions. The word does not carry the same weight as commandments, which they are. When someone tells me these are the beatitudes, I feel no conviction to follow them. They just feel like things that nice people do. However, saying they are commandments from Jesus about His kingdom, and that we must obey them to enter Heaven, carries a great conviction. Let us stop belittling His instructions and call them what they are... commandments... Kingdom commandments.

Let's take a closer look at them now.

Blessed are the poor in spirit: for theirs is the kingdom of Heaven. Blessed are they that mourn: for they shall be comforted.

This is not about being sad, depressed, or about literal mourning. It's about having our will subordinated by God's will. More precisely, it's about us submitting to God's will ahead of our personal gratification and desires. God is making a promise here that should we put him first, we shall reap a reward when it's all said and done. Apostle Paul said that if we only have hope in this life, we are of all men most miserable. This is what he was referring to. Our hope is not in this life. We are not supposed to place so much importance to this world that we forsake what is most important–life with Jesus in his Kingdom, after death, and the judgment.

Therefore, if this world offers us nothing but heartache and disappointment because we chose to live by God's standards rather than by man's, then we have hope.

If we experience misfortune after misfortune despite our faith in God, that's okay, because pleasures in heaven with Jesus are more important than pleasures in this life.

These words are Christ's commandments about "sticktoitiveness." He commands us that even to the point of pain, we are to stick with God, and he offers us a promise much the same way Mosaic law about honouring parents was the first commandment with a promise attached to it. We have a promise that He cares for us and will take care of us when the smoke clears. Fight the good fight of faith and lay hold onto salvation. Let's guard our hearts lest we be discouraged and lose out on the promise that is to come.

Blessed are the meek: for they shall inherit the earth.

Meekness means that we are <u>not</u> to put the interest of others below our interests. We are to be slow to fight when we feel challenged. Meekness is about relationships with others, often when we are in a position of strength. Meekness often requires us to put down our powers to defend ourselves, put down our power to inflict punishment on others, and it often requires us to put down our ability to exact justice against others. Meekness is a commandment, also with a promise. It's not optional. We don't get to choose when and to whom we are to be meek. After all, Jesus asked, do not the Gentiles do such things?

Luke 22:25-27 (KJV) ²⁵And he said unto them, The kings of the Gentiles exercise lordship over them; and they that exercise authority upon them are called benefactors. ²⁶But ye shall not be so: but he that is greatest among you, let him be as the younger; and he that is chief, as he that doth serve. ²⁷For whether is greater, he that sitteth at meat, or he that serveth? Is not he that sitteth at meat? But I am among you as he that serveth.

We may not all be kings, leaders, or bosses, but most of us have areas of our lives where we sit in a position of strength. It may not be on the job, but it could be when we go home as mothers and fathers. Older children often exercise leadership over younger; younger children grow up, and they exercise power over even younger kids and babies. At some point or another, most of us, if not all, are put in a place of power. The resounding question is, "are you meek?" or put another way, "do you rule with humility, as if you are a servant?"

Blessed are they which do hunger and thirst after righteousness: for they shall be filled.

Hunger for righteousness: This is about more than just hunger for spiritual things. Hunger for spiritual things might incorporate things like hunger for knowledge, or hunger for blessings. No, this is about hunger for righteousness. This means having a hunger to do the right thing, seeking out what is right and doing it, even when it's not necessary, or when others will not see what you have done. It's about doing what is right, even when it will be to your personal disadvantage. It's about a perfect combination of justice, judgment and mercy.

In this, Jesus teaches us not only to be righteous but to hunger after it. The pursuit of doing the right thing should be like our pursuit for food. Even if we fast, our bodies crave food. In fact, we can't live without it. So is doing what is right in God's eyes. We are commanded to do what is right—no deliberation or contemplation. No self-justification. No, "the end justifies the means." We are commanded to do what is right.

Blessed are the merciful: for they shall obtain mercy.

Be merciful: We are encouraged to be merciful, not to just have compassion, not to just care about others, and not to just have empathy. It's an action command. We are to BE merciful.

Later in His teachings during the Sermon on the Mount, Jesus taught his disciples how to pray. One part of the prayer is, "forgive us our debts as we forgive our debtors." In The Bahamas, as youngsters, we used an expression "shop closed." This was a cute way to say no. It meant that you would not be able to get whatever you want or need because the proverbial "shop is closed." We all need God's mercy and forgiveness, but if we choose not to be merciful or to forgive others...shop closed!

Blessed are the pure in heart: for they shall see God.

What makes our hearts pure? Certainly nothing that we do of ourselves. A pure heart is a heart that follows after God. The reference to pure in heart is taken from the old testament where God promised to give us a heart of flesh:

Ezekiel 36:26 (KJV) A new heart also will I give you, and a new spirit will I put within you: and I will take away the stony heart out of your flesh, and I will give you an heart of flesh.

This scripture prophetically spoke about the Holy Spirit and links the Holy Spirit to the commandments of the Kingdom and the promise of being heirs of God, as the Prophet continues (words in brackets inserted):

> *Ezekiel 36:27-28 (KJV) [27]And I will put my spirit (Holy Spirit) within you, and cause you to walk in my statutes, and ye shall keep my judgments (Commandments), and do them. [28]And ye shall dwell in the land that I gave to your fathers; and ye shall be my people, and I will be your God (Children of God).*

Such a heart needs the Holy Spirit as prophesied, and this is consistent with Jesus' statement in John 3:3 that one must be born of the Spirit otherwise, they will not see God.

Blessed are the peacemakers: for they shall be called the children of God.

BE peacemakers: This is another action commandment about relationships with others. Being peacemakers carries with it a greater expectation and understanding than simply not being a brawler or a fighter. It's not passive. It connotes actively trying to pursue peace. In today's world, we are often faced with differences of opinion, and some of them can be very testy and trying of our faith. Wars start because individuals are not prepared to be peacemakers. With God, this is a commandment.

Followers of Christ have lots of history with disagreements. Even in the early church, there were many examples of disagreements. Paul and Barnabas had such a major disagreement that they had to be separated–they couldn't work together. Then Paul faced off with Peter because he felt that Peter was not following his own revelation about God's acceptance of the Gentiles. In his letter to the Corinthians, Paul talked about people in the church having lawsuits against each other:

> *1 Corinthians 6:7 (KJV) Now therefore there is utterly a fault among you, because ye go to law one with another. Why do ye not rather take wrong? Why do ye not rather suffer yourselves to be defrauded?*

Too often, we fail at this command. Sadly, we disregard Christ's command and opt to fight for our "rights," much the same way the Corinthians did. Unfortunately, fighting is not a command, and we, therefore, should think twice, yeah thrice about this command before our next fight, even if it means that we accept being wrongly defrauded.

Blessed are they which are persecuted for righteousness' sake: for theirs is the kingdom of Heaven. Blessed are ye, when men shall revile you, and persecute you, and shall say all manner of evil against you falsely, for my sake.

Do right, even when it means that you must suffer for it. This is not just about persecution, but persecution for doing the right thing. There are no thanks here for being persecuted when you're guilty. Unfortunately, that's expected. But when we suffer for doing the right thing, when we suffer for telling the truth, when we suffer for helping others, when we suffer for keeping all of these commandments, we are blessed.

Other commandments

In the following sections, we summarize the remaining Kingdom commandments found in the Kingdom Sermon on the Mount. You will observe in them how Jesus raised the standards above that of the Mosaic Laws and the traditions of the Jewish Elders. When He said that our righteousness must exceed that of the Scribes and Pharisees, He meant it!

Anger (Matthew 5: 21-26)

Jesus commanded us to not to be angry with our brothers and sisters **without a cause**. We are to consider problems with others so highly that we are not to offer sacrifices at the altar if we know that someone has an issue with us. We must, at least, try to resolve those issues **first**. Although it may be a common practise, **Christ does not permit us to offend others in the name of being frank and honest.** Here, Jesus is teaching us that if we offend others, it is important that we fix it urgently because this kind of offense could land us in hell's fire. Paul in Ephesians 4:26-27 said: "Be ye angry, and sin not: **let not the sun go down upon your wrath**: Neither give place to the devil." This reiterates that we are commanded not to allow anger to remain in our hearts. We must not let too much time go by with anger in our hearts as this gives room for the devil to sneak in and attack us, and possibly, the people we are angry with.

I have heard many people say that it's okay to be angry once you don't act on it. Apparently, Apostle Paul did not share this view, and neither did Jesus. Moses set the original bar for being angry. The bar stopped just shy of murder. Jesus raised the bar, saying that we ought not be angry without a cause.

Lust (Matthew 5:27-30)

Adultery is a sin! Moses established this in the Laws, and Jesus did not change this dynamic. However, He clarified what adultery is. Adultery generally was deemed to mean physical, sexual intercourse between persons not lawfully married to the other party. This definition left other forms of sexual interaction vague. Because of our sinful nature and the manipulation of our deceitful enemy, mankind has come up with all kinds of sexual experiences that may not fall in the traditional definition of adultery. For example, some may think it's okay to look at a woman (or man) in a sexual way, as long as they don't touch her/him. Others may think they can use graphic pictures, videos, and audios to help them pleasure themselves because these also do not involve physical interaction with others.

Jesus had a different standard. He swept these and many other actions in His definition of adultery. He is saying that sin occurs in the heart rather than in the action. In Matthew 15:19-20, He said:

Matthew 15:19-20 (KJV) ¹⁹For out of the heart proceed evil thoughts, murders, **adulteries**, *fornications, thefts, false witness, blasphemies: ²⁰**These are the things which defile a man***

It's in the heart! Jesus, therefore, in His commandment to us, insists that we are not to lust after a woman or man because lust starts in the heart.

Abstinence is great, but in order to be in conformity with His commandments, we have to take an even greater stand regarding adultery and fornication. It's simply not enough to abstain from the physical act of fornication or adultery. We have to abstain from lust as well, and lust includes a multitude of sexual indiscretions.

Divorce (Matthew 5:31-32)

Divorce is a very sensitive and complicated subject matter, even during Jesus' lifetime. Three of the gospels (Matthew, Mark, and Luke) provide references to what Jesus said about it. Mark seems to have the most comprehensive recollection.

Mark 10:2-12 (NLT) ²Some Pharisees came and tried to trap him with this question: "Should a man be allowed to divorce his wife?" ³Jesus answered them with a question: "What did Moses say in the law about divorce?" ⁴"Well, he permitted it," they replied. "He said a man can give his wife a written notice of divorce and send her away." [5] *But Jesus responded,* **"He wrote this commandment only as a concession to your hard hearts.** [6] *But 'God made them male and female' from the beginning of creation.* [7] *This explains why a man leaves his father and mother and is joined to his wife,* [8] *and the two are united into one.'* **Since they are no longer two but one,** [9] **let no one split apart what God has joined together."** [10] *Later, when he was alone with his disciples in the house, they brought up the subject again.* [11] *He told them,* **"Whoever divorces his wife and marries someone else commits adultery against her.** [12] **And if a woman divorces her husband and marries someone else, she commits adultery."**

Jesus started with God's original intent for marriage. He explained, God views marriage as a joining of a man and a woman, and He never intended for that union to be broken by anyone for any reason. Moses, being compassionate to the struggles married people face, allowed a man to divorce his wife by writing a bill of divorcement. But Jesus was very clear that this was not God's original intent.

The disciples weren't satisfied with this. In fact, they seemed distraught. Matthew's recollection adds the text 'Jesus' disciples then said to him, "If this is the case, it is better not to marry!"' (Matthew 19:10 NLT). Mark only says that they brought it up again. Jesus, seemingly sympathetic to the difficulties people face in marriages, made His own allowances for divorce. However, He tightened Moses' rule by putting in a condition where divorce is allowed. Moses didn't have any conditions. Anyone could divorce for any reason. Jesus only allowed divorce for cases involving fornication by a partner. The person who divorces for any other reason and remarries commits adultery, whether it's the man or woman. Remarriage, therefore, is permitted by Jesus only for the person who divorces because of fornication.

There are other extenuating circumstances that should be considered when discussing divorce. For example:

- What about the person who was unsaved when they got divorced then remarried before they accepted Jesus as Lord of their life?

- What about the person who divorced because of abuse?

- What about the person who wanted to remain married, but their spouse decided to divorce them?

There are, no doubt, many other experiences that make this subject even more complicated for us to adjudicate as humans. In my humble opinion, the key question is what did Jesus mean by fornication, since this was the only exemption that He allowed. Was He being prescriptive, or was He generalizing? Did He literally mean for that only to include fornication, or did He mean for it to include other forms of unfaithfulness? Consider the following:

When Jesus faced the Samaritan woman at Jacob's well, He gave us a practical example of His position. He told her the following:

*John 4:10 (NIV) "If you knew the gift of God and who it is that asks you for a drink, you would have asked him **and he would have given you living water.**"*

The woman had five husbands (verse 18), yet Jesus was offering her salvation (living water). He was not perturbed by her previous divorces. He was still prepared to receive her into His Kingdom. Admittedly, we don't know her exact circumstances. It's possible that all of her husbands committed fornication, thus permitting her to remarry. However, Jesus seemed to suggest that she was adulterous when He said that the person she was currently with was not her husband (verse 18). Either way, we know that Jesus was ready to offer her His gift of life.

It's also interesting that Jesus used the word fornication (Greek "porneia") to describe the sin that allowed for a married person to divorce their spouse without committing adultery (Greek "moicháō"). If He literally meant having sex with another person, then that would be adultery (moicháō), rather than fornication (porneia). Strong's defines porneia as "harlotry (including adultery and incest); figuratively, idolatry:—fornication." Note that the definition includes more than adultery. Further, it literally implies severe behaviour, including illicit sex and idolatry. It seems that Jesus intentionally used this word to incorporate severe acts against a spouse.

Jesus is definitely sympathetic to those of us who struggle with God's original commandment regarding divorce. He clearly allowed us a limited exemption from what He knew was not God's original intention. However, marriage remains a very serious contract that should not be entered into lightly. It is intended to be irrevocable…until death do us part, and persons should only enter into it if they are prepared to live by this vow.

Swearing (Matthew 5:33-37)

As bad as some persons may think curse words may be, Jesus was not speaking about them. He was speaking about making oaths, and He commands us not to do it.

Whether or not you fulfill the oath is immaterial. Don't swear at all because you have no power over anything that you might place in the oath. Heaven is God's throne. The earth is His footstool. You have no control over your own body, not even so much as to control the natural colour of your hair. Therefore, if we have no true ownership or control over anything, we ought not to swear at all.

Concerning curse words, there are many other scriptures to consider. You be the judge.

Matthew 15:18 (KJV) But those things which proceed out of the mouth come forth from the heart; and they defile the man.

Matthew 12:36-37 (KJV) 36But I say unto you, That every idle word that men shall speak, they shall give account thereof in the day of judgment. 37For by thy words thou shalt be justified, and by thy words thou shalt be condemned.

Ephesians 4:29 (KJV) Let no corrupt communication proceed out of your mouth, but that which is good to the use of edifying, that it may minister grace unto the hearers.

James 36-12 (KJV) 6And the tongue is a fire, a world of iniquity: so is the tongue among our members, that it defileth the whole body, and setteth on fire the course of nature; and it is set on fire of hell. 7For every kind of beasts, and of birds, and of serpents, and of things in the sea, is tamed, and hath been tamed of mankind: 8But the tongue can no man tame; it is an unruly evil, full of deadly poison. 9Therewith bless we God, even the Father; and therewith curse we men, which are made after the similitude of God. 10Out of the same mouth proceedeth blessing and cursing. My brethren, these things ought not so to be. 11Doth a fountain send forth at the same place sweet water and bitter? 12Can the fig tree, my brethren, bear olive berries? Either a vine, figs? So can no fountain both yield salt water and fresh.

Retribution (Matthew 5:38-42)

This is a tricky command because it seems to fly against the scriptures that indicate that we are to be fair and just. If someone does us wrong, shouldn't we be able to defend ourselves and get retribution from the one who wronged us? As it turns out, this logic is carnal because it does not factor equally important scriptures about love and mercy. If we look inward-out the way that God wants us to, we will better appreciate that justice means that we should be just and fair <u>to others</u>. Asking for justice for ourselves in the manner that Moses taught (eye for an eye) is looking outward-in. When we are wronged, Jesus commands us to turn the other cheek, give our cloak, go the extra mile and give when we are asked.

Jesus is our chief example of taking abuse wrongfully and not allowing anger to fester in our hearts. Even the best of us today once lived in sin and disobedience to God. But His love for us continued notwithstanding. If we are comfortable accepting His forgiveness and patience with us, then we must do the same with others. We must turn the other cheek. We must forgive, otherwise, we will not be forgiven by God (Matthew 6:15).

Love our enemies (Matthew 5:43-48)

This commandment has multiple layers of responses that are to govern our behaviour toward persons who curse us, hate us, despitefully use us, and persecute us. First, we should love them. Then we should do good to them. Finally, we should pray for them. This, Jesus says, separates us as children of God. Try it! I guarantee that you will experience a spiritual euphoria that is unmatched. It is the high from knowing that you followed God's command even when it was difficult.

More Commandments

Jesus continued to establish and teach His Kingdom commandments throughout the Kingdom Sermon on the Mount, continuing even into chapters 6 and 7.

Almsgiving (Matthew 6:1-4)

In Matthew 6, Jesus taught us that we should **give alms privately** rather than self-promoting our almsgiving by announcing them to others. A closer look at this reveals that He is giving us two commandments wrapped into one. First, that we must give alms; and second, that we do it privately. Contrary to many person's beliefs, nowhere does Jesus teach us to give in order to be rewarded in <u>this</u> life. That's because doing this is like looking outward-in, which we have learned already, is not like God. As you will see, He teaches us to focus on our reward in Heaven. We will expound on this later.

Prayer (Matthew 6:5-15)

It's important to note that Jesus commands us to pray. One of the better-known parables that He preached about prayer is found in Luke 18:1-8. It's referred to as the Parable of the Unjust Judge. The moral of the parable is summed in verse 1: "And he spake a parable unto them to this end, **that men ought always to pray, and not to faint**." It is reinforced in verse 7, "And shall not God avenge his own elect, which cry day and night unto him, though he bear long with them?" Prayer, therefore, is something we must do and do continuously. Our prayer motto should be "Keep on Praying!"

There are also many scriptural references whereby Jesus prayed.

- Luke 3:21
- Matthew 14:23
- Mark 6:46
- Luke 6:12
- Mark 1:35
- Luke 5:16
- Matthew 26:36; 42 & 44
- Luke 11:1

Prayer was so important to Jesus that He gave us instructions on how to pray. He instructed us not to use vain repetitions as a means to prolong our prayers. It's not about the length of time, nor volumes of words. As Jesus explained in Matthew 6:8, "...for your Father knoweth what things ye have need of, before ye ask him." He already knows, there's no need to convince Him.

Jesus also commanded us not to pray to be seen, but instead to pray privately (in our closets and shut the door). After all, this was Jesus' MO when it came to His prayer life. In almost all of the above scriptures, you will find that Jesus went somewhere private to pray. This is partly the reason His disciples had to ask Him to teach them how to pray. Prayer is between God and us. Jesus Himself was very private with His prayers. This, however, does not mean that public prayer, like in church service, is wrong. Jesus is not condemning that; He is only teaching us the art of a personal prayer life.

As a part of His prayer model in verses 9 to 13 of Matthew 6 (The Lord's Prayer), Jesus touched on the following:

- Verse 9–Honouring God
- Verse 10–Following God's ways
- Verse 11–Our physical needs
- Verse 12–Receiving and giving forgiveness
- Verse 13–Keep us from the evil one
- Verse 13–Reminder that everything we do is for God's glory

Jesus highlighted something very important at the end of The Lord's Prayer. In verses 14 and 15, Jesus made sure we understood that we would not be forgiven by God if we do not forgive others. This is important because forgiving others is an attribute of God. Remember Exodus 34:6-7 when God explained to Moses what His character is like? God told Him that He is merciful, gracious, longsuffering, full of goodness and truth and that **He forgives iniquity, transgressions, and sin**. If we are to be like God (His image), we must forgive. However, Jesus raised the stakes for us by stating that if we don't forgive others, we will not be forgiven by God. Since we all need God's forgiveness, we all must forgive others also.

In truth, the last part of The Lord's Prayer may be the most important part. We must do everything to bring honour to God. This is how we get close to God, but it's also how we defeat the enemy. When Jesus was tempted in the wilderness for 40 days (Matthew 4), the Bible records three specific attacks from the devil. It is readily apparent that in all three, Jesus retorted with scriptures. However, what is often unnoticed is that all of the scriptures reveal WHY he did not yield to the devil. All showed that it was because He wanted to honour God.

In the first temptation (turn bread out of stones), Jesus' mind was on pleasing God. His response was that man must live by following the words of God. In other words, He honoured God by putting God first.

In His second temptation (prove He was God's son), Jesus responded that we must not tempt the Lord God. He was not talking about the devil tempting God. He was saying that He will not tempt God. He knew who He was in God; therefore, He would not tempt God by asking God to prove Himself. Incidentally, this is what the children of Israel did when they were in the wilderness. They tempted God by asking Him to prove that He was with them. We are never to tempt God. This reflects a lack of faith.

God is most supreme and powerful. Believe it, and never tempt Him with unbelief. Let's stop asking Him to prove Himself to us.

In the third temptation (worship satan), Jesus responded that we are only to worship God.

In every one of these temptations, Jesus showed how He focused on pleasing God. No wonder God said of Him in Matthew 3:17 and Matthew 17:5 that He is well-pleased with Jesus.

Fasting (Matthew 6:16-18)

Fasting is the third consecutive Kingdom commandment that Jesus gave that has two elements attached to it. First, that we should fast, and second, that when we do fast, we must not use it as an occasion to show others how spiritual we are by disfiguring ourselves so that we can be seen to have fasted. Jesus spoke about fasting more than once. He was once asked by John the Baptist's disciples why His disciples didn't fast. Read His response below:

*Matthew 9:15 (KJV) And Jesus said unto them, Can the children of the bridechamber mourn, as long as the bridegroom is with them? **But the days will come, when the bridegroom shall be taken from them, and then shall they fast.***

Jesus was saying that while they may not fast now, in the end, His disciples, too, will fast.

In chapter 17:14-21, Matthew recounts the importance of fasting. He wrote about the occasion when Jesus' disciples could not cure a possessed boy. Jesus called them faithless and perverse because they could not cure the boy. He didn't mean they were wicked, but that they still did not understand the lessons that He was teaching them; things about spiritual order and the heavenly power structure. These are things that they eventually got, but at that time, they did not understand them. In these words, Jesus was signifying that they still had very weak prayer and fasting lives and that it was a hindrance to their faith and spiritual development. Jesus said, "...this kind goeth not out but by prayer and fasting." We also have to fast!

If we consider these last three kingdom commandments together (almsgiving, prayer and fasting), it is certain that Jesus does not want us to be boastful about our spiritual commitments. He wants us to do them privately, between God and us. This needs to be reconciled with His commandment to let our lights shine before men. When talking about letting our lights shine before men, Jesus was referring to interpersonal interactions; in other words, things that require us to be humble, meek, peacemakers, suffer persecution falsely, etc. When faced with these relational issues, we must let our lights shine before men for them to see our good works and glorify our Father in Heaven. However, with regard to these three commandments, to the extent possible, Jesus wants us to make these personal experiences with God. He wants us to do them as privately as we can because when we do them privately with Him, we are in effect doing them for Him. Consider what Jesus said in Matthew 25:35-40 (KJV):

> *35For I was hungred, and ye gave me meat: I was thirsty, and ye gave me drink: I was a stranger, and ye took me in: 36Naked, and ye clothed me: I was sick, and ye visited me: I was in prison, and ye came unto me. 37Then shall the righteous answer him, saying, Lord, when saw we thee an hungred, and fed thee? Or thirsty, and gave thee drink? 38When saw we thee a stranger, and took thee in? Or naked, and clothed thee? 39Or when saw we thee sick, or in prison, and came unto thee? 40And the King shall answer and say unto them, Verily I say unto you, **Inasmuch as ye have done it unto one of the least of these my brethren, ye have done it unto me**.*

Wealth (Matthew 6:19-24)

Jesus commands us not to focus on worldly and financial success. Instead, He instructs us to lay treasures up in Heaven. He understands that we are all about building success and wealth on earth, and He understands the need for it. So much of our lives are centred around this. Many of us go to university to develop and prepare ourselves for success. We invest our money to grow our wealth. We build homes from our worldly and financial success. All of these are treasures that we build (or lay-up) on earth. If we follow Jesus' commandments concerning treasures, we will use the same energy to lay treasures in Heaven, and we would do it deliberately by following His commandments.

How do we lay treasures in Heaven? When we give to the poor, this is how we build an extension on our mansion in Heaven. When we pray for our enemies, we upgrade our old broken-down car in Heaven to a spanking new top of the line vehicle. When we turn the other cheek, we add a beautiful pool in the back of our mansion in Heaven. Yes, these are ridiculous concepts, but they illustrate two things: First, they show how we lay treasures in Heaven–i.e., by following the Kingdom commandments; and second, that we should be deliberate about building treasures in Heaven. We will get into much more details on wealth, money, and finances in Section 3.

Food, Clothes & Shelter (Matthew 6:25-34)

Jesus continued His Kingdom commandments, letting us know where to prioritize these basic needs that we have. We are to seek God's Kingdom first! We are to also rely on the fact that God loves us and knows that we have need of these things and that He will give them to us because of His love for us. He doesn't do it because we sow seed. He does it because He loves us. If He gives to us because we sow seed, then those persons with more seed (wealth) have a better chance to be blessed than persons with nothing at all. This would make God partial to the wealthy, which the scripture is abundantly clear that He is not. We will cover this subject at great length in Section 3.

Judging others (Matthew 7:1-5)

We are commanded not to judge others, especially since none of us are perfect. Because of this, we should be more concerned about being judged by others as a preventative measure of us judging others.

Golden Rule (Matthew 7:6-12)

Do unto others as you will have them do unto you. This is the golden rule and it is what Jesus commands us to honour. We all want to be respected and treated well. What Jesus is commanding us is that if we want to receive good treatment, we should treat others the way we want to be treated. If we want to be respected, we should first respect others. If we want to be forgiven, we must forgive others.

Warnings

In wrapping up the Kingdom Sermon on the Mount, Jesus gave us warnings of what would happen if we do not keep the Kingdom commandments that He outlined in the Kingdom Sermon. First, He warned that we must enter in by the strait gate and narrow way. He said that this is the way that leads to life, and few people find it. This means that **the strait gate and narrow way must be <u>found</u>**. If we are not looking for it, we will not find it. It's not something that we just stumble on. What we, in fact, stumble on is the wide gate and broad way. If we fail to look for the strait gate, we automatically are walking through the broad gate. Unfortunately, **it is the broad gate, Jesus says, that leads to destruction**.

Second, Jesus warns us to beware of false prophets. We must not follow them. How will we know them? By their fruit. Verse 19 says, **"Every tree that bringeth not forth good fruit is hewn down, and cast into the fire."** This means that **we don't have to be evil, to be evil**. Being evil is the absence of being good, so the watermark for being evil is very low. Just be human, and we will achieve evil. The next warning crystallizes this.

Third, Jesus warns that not everyone who does great things in the name of Jesus will enter into Heaven. He is warning us not to focus on works, but to focus on following His Kingdom commandments. If we love Him, He wants us to keep His commandments (John 14:15). There are many philanthropists in the world. Many rich people give away millions for great causes. Politicians do many good deeds to help persons who can't help themselves because they lack resources. Parishioners routinely give money and time to their church. All of these are highly commendable, and truly, they represent some of the characteristics of God. Benevolence is something that God demands of us. Here's what John said in his first letter:

> *1 John 3_16-17 (KJV)* *[16]Hereby perceive we the love of God, because he laid down his life for us: and we ought to lay down our lives for the brethren. [17]**But whoso hath this world's good, and seeth his brother have need, and shutteth up his bowels of compassion from him, how dwelleth the love of God in him?***

We know God loves us because He sacrificed His life for us. Love constrains us to do the same for others. John went on to explain unequivocally, that anyone who has been blessed with wealth and other goods and does not help those who are not, does not have the love of God in him and therefore is not aligned with God. However, doing good deeds is not good enough. We cannot buy God's favour with money and deeds. So, the underlying theme of this third warning is the following: **Doing good deeds is not enough to inherit the Kingdom of God, but not doing good, will prevent us**.

Jesus' warnings were similar, in intent, to the warnings that Moses gave in Deuteronomy. Moses was so repetitive about the need for Israel to obey God that he could almost be described as obsessive-compulsive. Jesus also warns us about disobedience. However, instead of the many penalties by way of the curses which Moses catalogued in Deuteronomy 28, Jesus laid out the one penalty for not following His commandments at the end of Matthew 7. The penalty is that we will not be allowed to enter the Kingdom of Heaven. No more will persons be punished with earthly plagues and problems for refusing Him and, by extension, God. He confirms His love and favour even for those whom He considers evil and unjust in Matthew 5:44-48. Heaven is our prize! The consolation "prize" is our destruction. That is the ultimate penalty at the end of each warning that Jesus gave.

He makes it clearer in Matthew7:24-27, that those of us who keep His commandments are like a house built on a rock which is able to withstand all of the challenges it faces and, in the end, to remain standing. On the other hand, everyone who does not keep His commandments will fall like a house built on sand. Great, Jesus admonishes, will be the fall of those who do not keep His commandments.

The People's Response

At the end of the Kingdom Sermon on the Mount, the people appreciated that He had just established something new...a new doctrine; new commandments.

Matthew 7:28-29 (KJV) ²⁸And it came to pass, when Jesus had ended these sayings, the people were astonished at his doctrine: ²⁹For he taught them as one having authority, and not as the scribes.

Matthew added this line to make it clear to everyone that all of the preceding words were part of His Kingdom doctrine. He could easily have ended this story with the warnings. He didn't because he wanted to reiterate the importance of the moment. Jesus had just established something really great. He established His Kingdom commandments.

PERSONAL APPLICATION

The new testament authors wrote about the same principles found in the Kingdom Sermon on the Mount. I challenge Readers to compare the teachings of the new testament writers to this Sermon. You will find, just as I have, that the messages are the same. Below, I arbitrarily selected the book of James to show the similarities.

James made reference to the "law of liberty" twice (James 1:25 and James 2:12). There is no other reference to this in the Bible, therefore this seems to be a phrase that James coined himself. It's really nice and has a ring of lawyerly legalese to it. Was he talking about the Mosaic Laws, or the Kingdom Laws as outlined above? James used the word 'law' 10 times in his epistle. He talked about the perfect law, the royal law and the law of liberty. There's no reason to believe these are different laws. But the question remains; was he referring to Moses or Jesus? The answer lies in James 4:12 where he says there is one lawgiver and qualifies it with "who is able to save and destroy." Moses was able to do neither of these, therefore it's safe to conclude James was referring to Jesus' laws. Let's take a look at what he talked about in the book of James.

Chapter 1

1. He advised them how to deal with temptations, i.e. by being patient. (See Matthew 6:13)

2. He reminded them to ask for things in faith, but not to waiver because wavering is what causes us not to receive what we ask for from the Lord. (See Matthew 7:7)

3. He encouraged people who were "of low degree" (meaning poor) that they were exalted, presumably in Christ. (See Matthew 6:24)

4. He explained the transitory nature of wealth. (See Matthew 6:19-20)

5. He even explained how temptations work to help his readers both understand and defeat it. (See Matthew 6:13)

6. He advised them not to be angry. (See Matthew 5:22)

7. He encouraged them to be meek. (See Matthew 5:5)

8. He taught them not to offend others by their words. (See Matthew 5:22)

9. He advised them to help those that are in need (fatherless and motherless). (See Matthew 5:42)

Chapter 2

1. He told them not to be partial in their dealings with the rich above the poor. (See Matthew 5:46-47)

2. He told them to love their neighbours as themselves. (See Matthew 5:44)

3. He reminded them that if they do not show mercy, they will not receive mercy in the judgment from God. (See Matthew 6:15)

4. He encouraged them to help the poor and needy. (See Matthew 5:42)

Chapter 3

1. Again, he reminded them about controlling their tongues. (See Matthew 5:37)

2. He reminded them about being meek. (See Matthew 5:5)

3. He summarized the important traits that we are to demonstrate in our lives–"pure, then peaceable, gentle, and easy to be intreated, full of mercy and good fruits, without partiality, and without hypocrisy." (See Matthew 5:3-10)

Chapter 4

1. He warned them about their internal fighting with each other. (See Matthew 5:9)

2. He confirmed that it's okay to mourn and weep and to humble ourselves. (See Matthew 5:4)

3. He chided anyone who judges others. (See Matthew 7:1)

4. He explained why we should seek God rather than wealth, that it only lasts a little while then vanishes. (See Matthew 6:24)

Chapter 5

1. He demotes the concept of having gain on earth, especially when it is obtained through dishonesty. (See Matthew 6:22-23)

2. He promotes that we wait patiently for the Lord's return–He draweth nigh. (See Matthew 7:21)

3. He told them not to swear. (See Matthew 5:34)

4. Finally, he reminded them of the importance of prayer. (See Matthew 6:6)

If we were to juxtapose these with Jesus's Kingdom commandments in the Sermon on the Mount, it's clear that James was simply repeating the commandments that he heard and learned from Jesus and The Holy Spirit. That's why he called them the Law of Liberty, because following them can save and set us free.

James wasn't the only one who preached the Kingdom messages. The same can be said about Paul, Peter, Luke, John, Matthew and the rest. They all preached the same messages. Read them again and you will see that their messages were common and were about the Kingdom commandments of Jesus–the Perfect Law of Liberty. Because they all preached the same messages, it stands to reason that we ought to take this message seriously and not allow ourselves to be distracted by substitute doctrines emanating from charismatic orators, which have a form of godliness, but are inconsistent with the messages of Jesus.

If we hear messages that teach us to fight for something, be careful because Jesus teaches us to be peacemakers. If their messages teach us to pursue wealth and success, be careful because Jesus taught us that we cannot serve God and riches. If their messages teach us to give as a means to receive blessings, then shun it, because Jesus taught us to give, expecting nothing back in return.

Jesus warned us in the closing verses of the Kingdom Sermon on the Mount to "Beware of false prophets" (Matthew 7:15). We will know them by their fruit, is what He said. If they are teaching things that are inconsistent with what Jesus commanded us in the Sermon on the Mount, then they are false teachers and they should not be followed.

Patrick James McFall

Chapter 6

Kingdom Guide
(Holy Spirit)

GPS

Millions of visitors come to The Bahamas every year. Many are repeat visitors, but quite a lot are first-time visitors. Our capital city is Nassau (on the Island of New Providence), and it's a very small city (only 21 miles by 7 miles). Even in a small country like The Bahamas, and a small city like Nassau, it's impossible for tourists to survive without help. You need help finding your hotel, good restaurants, tourist attractions, the best shopping malls and plazas, our wonderful Bahamian handicraft, and of course, you need help finding our lovely turquoise beaches, and that's what most visitors come to The Bahamas for–sun, sand and sea. You can certainly try to do it on your own. The Bahamas is a free democratic country, and we value our guests very highly. Those who want privacy can find it here, but even so, at some point, they too will need someone else. Even some of our best beaches won't be found without help.

The work of the Holy Spirit is similar, but this honestly barely scratches the surface of the importance of the Holy Spirit. To navigate God's Kingdom, God has given each of us a personal guide. He's given us all the same guide, the Holy Ghost who came from God and who, as a member of the Trinity, knows everything about the Kingdom there is to know. He knows each path, so to speak. He knows where to find pasture. He knows each street, valley, neighbourhood. He knows it all, and we, as children of God, have access to all of that knowledge through the Holy Spirit. We will not experience anything in God's Kingdom without Him.

Jesus once described himself as the door.

John 10:9 (KJV) ***I am the door***: *by me if any man enter in, he shall be saved and* ***shall go in and out, and find pasture***.

Using the same analogy, if Jesus is the door, then the Holy Spirit is the Guide who helps us find pasture in the unknown fields of the Kingdom. In John 14:26, Jesus called Him our Helper. He alone has that role. Jesus said the following in John 16:12-14 (KJV)

> *¹²I have yet many things to say unto you, **but ye cannot bear them now**. ¹³Howbeit when he, the Spirit of truth, is come, he will **guide you** into all truth: for he shall not speak of himself; but whatsoever he shall hear, that shall he speak: and he will shew you things to come. ¹⁴**He shall glorify me**: for **he shall receive of mine, and shall shew it unto you**.*

Jesus' time on earth as a human was limited. He was also limited by his human form. He was limited in His purpose for coming to earth as a human. Not to mention, He was limited by the readiness, or lack thereof, of His disciples. Basically, there was only so much He could do because of these limitations. He wanted to do more. He wanted to say more. But He couldn't because they simply weren't ready. Jesus was a little disappointed by this, but thanks be to God that He gave us the Holy Spirit to guide us and teach us the things that Jesus could not because of these limitations. **The only limitation that the Holy Spirit has to reveal the truth to us is us.**

However, as noted above, the work of the Holy Spirit is so much more than just being our Helper. In chapter 3 of John's gospel, Jesus expounded on how critical a role the Holy Spirit plays in God's Kingdom.

> *John 3:3-5 (KJV) ³Jesus answered and said unto him, Verily, verily, I say unto thee, **Except a man be born again, he cannot see the kingdom of God**. ⁴Nicodemus saith unto him, How can a man be born when he is old? Can he enter the second time into his mother's womb, and be born? ⁵Jesus answered, Verily, verily, I say unto thee, **Except a man be born of water and of the Spirit, he cannot enter into the kingdom of God**.*

I must confess that I once was so focused on the fact that Jesus said that we must be born again, that I overlooked His explanation of how one becomes born again. I thought it was only about repentance. However, Jesus explained this process to comprise two distinct parts–born of water and born of the Spirit. In Matthew 3:11, John the Baptist described his baptism this way: "I indeed baptize you with water unto repentance." Peter described the baptism of Jesus this way: "Repent, and be baptized every one of you in the name of Jesus Christ for the remission of sins" (Acts

2:38). **Water baptism is a symbol of repentance, whereby our sins are washed away.** It is the first part of Jesus' definition of "born again." There is a second part, which Jesus called born "of the Spirit." In this chapter, we will focus primarily on Spirit baptism, and as we shall see, **Spirit baptism is a symbol of adoption.** Jesus said that we cannot **see** nor **enter** into the Kingdom unless we are born of water AND the Spirit. Imagine that! We can't even see it much less enter into it. So, I was right; being born again is about repentance. However, we must also be born of the Spirit if we want to enter into God's Kingdom.

The above scripture is also key to understanding how vitally important the Holy Spirit is to the Kingdom. In Matthew 6:33, Jesus said that we are to **seek** the Kingdom of God and His righteousness first. This might be one of the most quoted scriptures in the Bible. We use this scripture to explain how important it is to put God first in our lives. We learn that we are to seek the Kingdom of God above things like food, raiment, and shelter. However, Jesus declared that we cannot even see the Kingdom without the Holy Spirit. **So then, there is a prerequisite to seeking the Kingdom of God first, and it is being born again, which, by definition, requires baptism of water and the Holy Spirit.** Since we need the Holy Spirit to guide and teach us about the Kingdom, attempting to find the Kingdom without the Holy Spirit is as futile as seeking something unfamiliar **and** invisible.

If we can't see the Kingdom without the Holy Spirit, then neither can we experience the Kingdom without Him. One might say that the Holy Spirit is, therefore, as vital to the Kingdom as Jesus. Through Jesus, we have salvation. That's why we must be baptised in the name of Jesus. However, it's important that we also fully understand that we must also be baptised in the Holy Spirit. This makes the Holy Spirit just as important to the Kingdom of God as Jesus. We need both of them if we want to see or enter the Kingdom of God. King Jesus is, therefore, not the only important person in the Kingdom. We must have the Holy Ghost too.

Quench Not the Spirit

One of the greatest travesties of the church occurs when we quench the Spirit. In 1 Thessalonians 5:19, the author said: "Quench not the Spirit." Also, in Ephesians 4:30, the writer says, "grieve not the holy Spirit of God." These two, along with several others, help us understand that we can minimize the Holy Spirit in our lives. I believe that we do these things (grieve and quench the Spirit) when we relegate Him to a back seat in our lives. The Holy Spirit is here to teach, to correct, and to guide us in the things of God. He leads us in the paths of righteousness. He is the dominant member of the Godhead on earth at this time. Each time we fail to acknowledge Him or fail to listen to Him or fail to follow His lead, we are, in fact, quenching the Holy Spirit.

However, sometimes quenching the Spirit is about failure to grow. As we noted earlier in This Book, anything that is not growing is decaying. We just quoted Ephesians 4:30 "grieve not the Holy Spirit." However, the entire dialog that preceded this verse was about the work of the Holy Spirit in perfecting the lives of the Saints (Ephesians 4:12). It starts with an admonition to walk worthy of the vocation whereby we are called (verse 1). Then the chapter continues to explain the work of the Holy Spirit in the development of the Believers. Grieving the Spirit is not only what happens when we commit deliberate acts of sin, some of which are listed in Ephesians 4, but it also happens when we refuse to grow and develop spiritually. The following verses encapsulates this point:

> *Ephesians 4:14-16 (KJV)* ¹⁴ ***That we henceforth be no more children***, *tossed to and fro, and carried about with every wind of doctrine, by the sleight of men, and cunning craftiness, whereby they lie in wait to deceive;* ¹⁵ ***But speaking the truth in love, may grow up into him in all things***, *which is the head, even Christ:* ¹⁶*From whom the whole body fitly joined together and compacted by that which every joint supplieth, according to the effectual working in the measure of every part, maketh increase of the body unto the edifying of itself in love.*

The Gospel did not end with Jesus

Jesus, wanting to make certain that we understand the importance of the Holy Spirit, declared that any sin committed by mankind may be forgiven, even blasphemy against Himself. However, blasphemy against the Holy Spirit would not be forgiven. At some level, it's almost as if Jesus was exalting the Spirit above Himself in this regard to help us understand how important the Spirit is. He did it again when He told His disciples that it is expedient for them that He leaves because if He does not leave, they cannot be filled with the Holy Ghost. As great as Jesus is, even being the promised Messiah that would save all mankind, He nevertheless made it a point to promote the importance of the Spirit to us.

The work of God's redemption did not end when He died and rose again, but this work continues with the Holy Spirit. The work of the Holy Spirit is just the next installment of the redemptive work to remake us in the image of God. The Holy Spirit, as part of that redemptive work, brings us into sonship with God.

Galatians 4:1-6 (KJV) Now I say, That the heir, as long as he is a child, differeth nothing from a servant, though he be lord of all; 2But is under tutors and governors until the time appointed of the father. 3Even so we, when we were children, were in bondage under the elements of the world: 4But when the fulness of the time was come, God sent forth his Son, made of a woman, made under the law, 5To redeem them that were under the law, that we might receive the adoption of sons. 6And because ye are sons, **God hath sent forth the Spirit of his Son into your hearts, crying, Abba, Father.**

We are saved by the death and resurrection of Jesus so that death has no more power over us. We are sealed as children of God because of the life-giving power of the Holy Spirit.

Ephesians 1:13-14 (KJV) 13In whom ye also trusted, after that ye heard the word of truth, the gospel of your salvation: in whom also after that ye believed, ye were sealed with that holy Spirit of promise. 14Which is the earnest of our inheritance until the redemption of the purchased possession, unto the praise of his glory.

We become children of God through Jesus. The Bible says that He gives as many of us as believes in Him the power to become a child of God (John 1:12). As a child of God, He sends His Spirit into our hearts. We also become heirs of God's promises once we become children of God. The Holy Ghost is described above as the earnest, or down payment, of our inheritance. These all speak to the fact that we cannot enter into God's Kingdom without the Holy Ghost.

There is no doubt that we cannot be with, nor please God, without the Holy Spirit.

Be Baptised

John the Baptist was the forerunner for Jesus, and his message was about repentance for the remission of sins. As the forerunner, John also preached about the Kingdom of Heaven. Matthew 3:2 expressly states that John told his listeners to repent for the Kingdom of Heaven was at hand. Luke 3 gives a more descriptive account of John's message. Luke recounted some of the specific things that John the Baptist taught about the Kingdom, and it should be of no surprise that John taught the same basic principles that Jesus did. There, in Luke 3, John taught Israel about giving to the poor (verse 11); being fair and just in their dealings with others (verse 13); being meek and not focusing on worldly wealth (verse 14); and other kingdom messages (verse 18) such as adultery (verse 19), so much so that Herod the tetrarch imprisoned and eventually killed John because of this message. No wonder Jesus said that from John the Baptist until now, the Kingdom of Heaven suffered violence and the violent taketh it by force. The world resisted the Kingdom commandments then, and it still resists it today.

Embedded in his message, John promoted baptism as the culmination of the act of repentance. Even in this, John's message was the same as Jesus'. Both preached repentance and baptism. As we very well know, John's baptism was with water signifying the cleansing from sin. On the other hand, Jesus baptised with the Holy Ghost and fire, just as John is quoted to have said in Matthew 3.

*Matthew 3:11 (KJV) I indeed baptize you with water **unto repentance**. but he that cometh after me is mightier than I, whose shoes I am not worthy to bear: **he shall baptize you with the Holy Ghost, and with fire:***

John prepared the way for Jesus by calling everyone to repentance. After repentance came water baptism and after water baptism came the baptism of the Holy Ghost. Here again, we see two baptisms. Despite the potential disagreement among Christian denominations, as to immerse or not to immerse, water baptism is easy enough to understand. It works hand in hand with repentance. But what of Spirit Baptism?

Baptism in the Spirit

We have already shared how important the Holy Spirit is. How then are we to be born or baptised in the Spirit, as Jesus said, we must? Jesus dispelled Nicodemus' silly question about entering a second time into our mother's womb. This is definitely not the way. It's pretty gross and somewhat insulting that he even asked about it. He obviously was asking out of sheer ignorance, or worse, facetiousness. Putting that aside, how then are we supposed to be born of the Spirit?

Baptism of the Holy Spirit has been debated for centuries by people of renown stature. Some of the world's greatest Bible scholars disagree on how we are baptised in the Spirit. We know already that there are two baptisms–baptism in the water and in the Spirit. Both baptisms were practised by the early saints. In Acts 19, Paul asked the Ephesian disciples if they received the Holy Ghost since (or after) they believed. They said no, and that they were only baptised with John's baptism. Paul explained that John baptised people who believed in Jesus. After this, Paul then baptised them in the name of Jesus and helped them receive (be baptised in) the Holy Ghost.

The same thing happened with Peter in Acts 8:14-17. Peter and John were sent to Samaria to pray for the disciples to receive the Holy Ghost. Prior to that, they were only baptised in the name of Jesus. Peter differentiated these baptisms again when the Gentiles were baptised in the Holy Ghost in Acts 10:44-48. After they were baptised in the Holy Ghost, Peter insisted that they also be baptised in water, thus ensuring that they received both baptisms.

On the day of Pentecost, a multitude heard the disciples speaking in tongues. After Peter spoke to them about the significance of what they were witnessing, they were pricked in their hearts and asked: "What shall we do?" Peter responded on this wise (text in parentheses added):

Acts 2:38-39 (KJV) ³⁸Then Peter said unto them, Repent, and be baptized (water baptism) every one of you in the name of Jesus Christ for the remission of sins, and ye shall receive the gift of the Holy Ghost (Spirit baptism). ³⁹For the promise is unto you, and to your children, and to all that are afar off, even as many as the Lord our God shall call.

The promise, Peter recalled, is for all of us. What promise? The gift of (baptism in) the Holy Ghost.

These scriptures leave no doubt about the difference between water baptism and baptism in the Holy Ghost. Water baptism is the culmination of repentance. However, there are many who believe that Christians receive or are baptised in the Holy Spirit the moment we receive Christ as Saviour. These scriptures in Acts of The Apostles definitely challenge this concept since, in all cases, the baptism of the Spirit occurred after salvation for these individuals. In their defense, proponents of this theory erroneously use the following scriptures in support of their assertions:

1 Corinthians 12:13 (KJV) For by one Spirit are we all baptized into one body, whether we be Jews or Gentiles, whether we be bond or free; and have been all made to drink into one Spirit.

Romans 8:9 (KJV) But ye are not in the flesh, but in the Spirit, if so be that the Spirit of God dwell in you. Now if any man have not the Spirit of Christ, he is none of his.

*Ephesians 1:13-14 (KJV) [13]In whom ye also trusted, after that ye heard the word of truth, the gospel of your salvation: in whom also **after that ye believed**, ye were sealed with that holy Spirit of promise, [14]Which is the earnest of our inheritance until the redemption of the purchased possession, unto the praise of his glory.*

The argument using 1 Corinthians is that Paul could not have said that we are all baptised into one body if every believer was not baptised in the Spirit. However, this argument is weak because it makes generalizations as to who is referred to as "we" when Paul said, "are we all baptised into one body." Paul could easily have only been referring to those persons whom he knew were actually baptised in the Spirit, as opposed to speaking about every believer.

The scripture in Romans is believed to be more conclusive to the proponents of concurrent baptisms. Paul said that anyone who does not have the Spirit of Christ is none of His. Therefore, they argue that once a person accepts Christ, they must have the Spirit of God. However, this conclusion is misguided. Jesus said that we cannot see nor enter the Kingdom of God unless we are baptised in both water and Spirit. Paul is saying the same thing–if we don't have the Spirit, we are none of Christ's, that is, we cannot enter God's Kingdom.

Finally, the Ephesians text is assumed to support the baptism at salvation principle because it states that we are sealed with the Spirit. However, this scripture makes the opposite assertion. It states that they were sealed **after they believed**. This is no misstatement because it's exactly how it happened. Our earlier scripture that we quoted about Paul and the Ephesians in Acts 19 confirms this fact. Paul asked them if they received the Spirit <u>after</u> they believed. The Holy Ghost came on the Ephesians after Paul laid hands on them, which happened after they believed (i.e. received salvation).

Consider also what happened between Peter and Simon in Acts 8. Peter laid hands on the believers in Samaria, and they received the Holy Ghost (Acts 8:17). Simon saw this and coveted this power. He offered to pay Peter and the disciples to be able to also lay hands on persons and have them receive the Holy Ghost (Acts 8:18-19). Peter rebuked him then made a statement that affirmed his position on this debate.

*Acts 8:20 (KJV) But Peter said unto him, Thy money perish with thee, because thou hast thought that **the gift of God** may be purchased with money.*

Peter called the power to lay hands on others in order for them to receive the Holy Ghost, a gift of God. Since receiving the Spirit is imparted as a gift, as Peter stated, then it would not be something that is automatically received at salvation. After all, what would be the point of giving someone a gift to impart something to everyone else who already has the thing that the gift purportedly imparts?

If the preponderance of the above is not sufficient, consider Jesus Christ Himself. The Bible teaches us that John was busy baptising others in the river Jordan, when one day, Jesus came to Him to be baptised. You can read different perspectives on this story in the four gospels. The gist of what happened is that Jesus went to John to be baptised. This is significant because He chose to submit himself to the same ordinance of water baptism. John, recognizing that Jesus was the Son of God at first refused to baptise Jesus, saying that he needed to be baptised by Jesus instead. However, Jesus told John that he must baptise Him in order to fulfill all righteousness. The fact that Jesus considered water baptism a part of God's righteousness is an important biblical principle. It suggests, rather strongly, that all Christians should be baptised in water.

In addition to confirming that water baptism is an act of righteousness, there are a few other important observations that we should note about this experience. We should not lose sight of the fact that Jesus chose to be baptised as an adult. We know that Jesus spent a lot of time around religious leaders in His youth. Regardless of any religious acts that He participated in during those years, He still chose, as a man, to be baptised in water. Additionally, Jesus was baptised in the river Jordan, suggesting that He was most likely immersed in the river as part of the baptism process.

After John baptised Jesus, the Holy Spirit came on Him (like a dove), and God spoke to Him. This is a manifestation of the baptism of the Spirit, and it was part and parcel of the righteousness which Jesus said must be fulfilled. It wasn't until this occurred that Jesus officially began His ministry. Therefore, Jesus left us an example that we must be both baptised in water and in the Holy Ghost. The truth is that Jesus did not need to be baptised in water nor the Spirit because He was without sin and was literally born of the Spirit. The Holy Ghost impregnated Mary with Jesus. His decision to be baptised in water and the Spirit was for us to see and know what is expected of us. We are to be baptised in water and Spirit!

The evidence

No matter what your beliefs are in this debate about the timing and circumstance that we receive the Holy Spirit, it is certain that salvation is not complete without the Holy Ghost. If we, therefore, have the Holy Spirit, how do we know for sure that we do? After all, He is a spirit, and we cannot see Him. Is there any way to know for sure that we have the Holy Ghost? Yes. Consider the following scripture.

*John 3:8 (KJV) The wind bloweth where it listeth, and thou hearest the sound thereof, **but canst not tell whence it cometh**, and whither it goeth: so is every one that is born of the Spirit.*

This is what Jesus told Nicodemus about the evidence of the birth (baptism) of the Spirit. The wind blows where it wants, and you will know it is blowing because you can hear it and see its effect. This tells me that while we may not be able to see it with our eyes, there will be evidence of the Holy Spirit in our lives, which will confirm those of us who are baptised in the Holy Spirit.

Sometimes this is confirmed by speaking in tongues. In the new testament, this was the primary evidence of the Spirit baptism. Acts 2:4 says:

Acts 2:4 (KJV) And they were all filled with the Holy Ghost and began to speak with other tongues, as the Spirit gave them utterance.

This was the first experience of the baptism of the Holy Spirit. More are recorded in Acts of The Apostles. In Acts 10:46, the house of Cornelius spoke in tongues. Acts 19:6 records the Christians in Ephesus speaking in tongues. In the early church, speaking in tongues was the predominant display of the evidence of the baptism of the Spirit. However, it doesn't appear to have been the only evidence, nor does it appear to have been a universal evidence for everyone. Paul asked the Corinthians, "do all speak in tongues?" suggesting that everyone may not. Therefore, no one should belittle a brother or sister for not speaking in tongues as if they are less holy or less righteous. Conversely, Paul also told the same Corinthians that he spoke in tongues more than all of them did. Clearly, he was not denigrating the act of speaking in tongues, and neither should anyone else.

Gifts

The Bible says in Ephesians 4:8 that Jesus gave gifts to men when He ascended on high. The gifts were given through the Holy Spirit and represent the thing or things that He wants us to do. Wikipedia summarizes the gifts of the Spirit in the following table:

Romans 12:6-8	1 Corinthians 12:8-10	1 Corinthians 12:28-30	Ephesians 4:11	1 Peter 4:11
1. Prophecy 2. Serving 3. Teaching 4. Exhortation 5. Giving 6. Leadership 7. Mercy	1. Word of wisdom 2. Word of knowledge 3. Faith 4. Gifts of healings 5. Miracles 6. Prophecy 7. Distinguishing between spirits 8. Tongues 9. Interpretation of tongues	1. Apostle 2. Prophet 3. Teacher 4. Miracles 5. Kinds of healings 6. Helps 7. Administration 8. Tongues	1. Apostle 2. Prophet 3. Evangelist 4. Pastor 5. Teacher	1. Whoever speaks 2. Whoever renders service

People who are baptised and filled with the Spirit demonstrate one or more of these gifts. However, be warned that not everyone who is gifted in these areas has the Holy Spirit. Some people are very gifted by God but fail, or maybe refuse, to use their gifts under the auspices of the Holy Spirit. Some people elect to pervert their gifts by promoting behaviours antithetical to God. This is all unfortunate but very true.

When Moses was commanded by God to lay his staff on the ground, and it turned into a snake, the Egyptian Sorcerers also laid down their staffs, and they too became snakes. There are false prophets and teachers today just as there were then. In his prolific sermon about the Kingdom (Sermon on the Mount), Jesus warned his disciples about false prophets (Matthew 7:15 - 20) and people who mimic those having the Holy Spirit (Matthew 7:21 – 23). But He was not only warning the disciples. He was also warning those engaged in such deception that in the end, they will not be accepted by God in His Kingdom (see verse 21 and 23). This warning is true even if our intention is not evil. We can only get into the Kingdom through Jesus and the Holy Ghost. Doing good deeds does not get us in.

PERSONAL APPLICATION
DON'T LOOK A GIFT HORSE IN THE MOUTH

The Holy Spirit gives us gifts. When we choose not to use the gifts, it is as if we are rejecting them. If we reject the gifts of the Spirit, we are rejecting Him. By rejecting The Holy Spirit, we are rejecting Jesus who sent Him to us, and this in turn is a repudiation of God.

There can be no other purpose for our existence as Christians than to do what God wants of us. This means that our purpose in life really is to allow the gift of the Holy Spirit to operate in our lives. We may have heard that our purpose is revealed in what we do well and what we are passionate about. While this may be true some of the times, consider that a significant part of Jesus' purpose was to suffer and die for our sins. Certainly, He could not be considered good at this because He only did it once. There is also evidence that He was not exactly passionate about it. He asked God to take the cup from Him if it were possible. Knowing that it was not possible, He accepted God's purpose and everything that went along with it. John also highlighted Jesus' struggle with His purpose in the Gospel of John chapter 12, verse 27. It reads:

"Now is my soul troubled; and what shall I say? Father, save me from this hour: but for this cause came I unto this hour. Father, glorify thy name."

Jesus admitted that His soul was troubled. He was nervous about what He was about to experience. This signifies that as Christians, we might not be very comfortable with our gifts. However, this scripture also reveals that we must put the purpose of God ahead of our personal interests where these are not aligned. Christ did it and so must we. God is glorified when we put His will above ours. That's why Jesus taught us to pray "Thy will be done." Our purpose is to yield to the Holy Spirit and this sometimes might not be the same as pursuing our greatest talents. For example, we might have a great singing talent, but God may call us to teach. This is important because God has a plan for us, and He knows how everyone fits into that plan. If we deviate from His plan in our attempt to follow our talents, no matter how successful we become in our talents, we will not be walking with God.

There is another reason it's important to fulfil our gifts. God designed it so that we cannot be perfected without each other. This is the conundrum of our interconnectivity. This is why it's so important that we give to each other, as we will learn in the next chapter. We must give because we cannot be perfected without receiving. That's why Jesus reaffirmed the Golden Rule in the Kingdom Sermon on the Mount when he said "Therefore all things whatsoever ye would that men should do to you, do ye even so to them: for this is the law and the prophets" (Matthew 7:12). It's inescapable. We need each other. Paul brilliantly said in 1 Corinthians 12:4-12:

> *⁴ Now there are diversities of gifts, but the same Spirit. ⁵And there are differences of administrations, but the same Lord. ⁶And there are diversities of operations, but it is the same God which worketh all in all. ⁷**But the manifestation of the Spirit is given to every man to profit withal.** ⁸For to one is given by the Spirit the word of wisdom; to another the word of knowledge by the same Spirit; ⁹To another faith by the same Spirit; to another the gifts of healing by the same Spirit; ¹⁰To another the working of miracles; to another prophecy; to another discerning of spirits; to another divers kinds of tongues; to another the interpretation of tongues: ¹¹**But all these worketh that one and the selfsame Spirit, dividing to every man severally as he will.** ¹²For as the body is one, and hath many members, and all the members of that one body, being many, are one body: so also is Christ.*

See the bolded verses. Take special note of them because it means that when we combine it with the fact that we are all given different gifts, when we withhold our gifts, we are disobeying God who commands that our gifts are for others to profit from. Disobedience is sin. We have no alternatives. We have no choice in the matter. We MUST allow the Holy Spirit to use us in His giftings.

Patrick James McFall

Section 3

Kingdom Finances

In this section, we explore God's truth about money and its purpose for Believers. We cover the role of the rich and the poor, so that no one is excluded. We also provide support to persons who need help with **personal budgeting, which along with hard work, charity, faith and God's providence, is the real secret to God's financial blessings**.

The preponderance of messages out there about money focuses on how we must position ourselves to be blessed with money. Many people, who attempt to teach about money from a Godly perspective, teach us what we need to do to get blessed. However, many of these things are incongruent with God's nature. Although Jesus taught many things about money, His message did not vary, nor did it deviate from God's nature. Although Jesus taught a lot about blessings and reward, the reward was always the same.

God certainly has an economic plan for His people. Its foundation is the same as we have learned about God thus far. God is great and self-sufficient. He does not need us for anything. Everything about our relationship with Him is one-sided. We are takers and He is a giver. We need Him for life, He needs us for nothing. He doesn't need our worship, our time, our money, our lives; He needs nothing from us. In fact, most of us are offensive to Him. We ignore Him. We disregard the things that He commands us to do, and we do the things He commands us not to do. Yet He elects to be merciful, gracious, longsuffering, plenteous in goodness and truth, keeping mercy for thousands, and forgiving iniquity, transgression, and sin (Exodus 34:6-7).

In the last chapter, we shared about the importance of the Holy Spirit. His job (if you want to call it that), is to help us become more like God. He re-establishes God's image in us by helping us live according to God's standards. Therefore, if we are led by the Spirit, we will exhibit God's personality traits. Apostle Paul called them the fruit of the Spirit in Galatians 5:22-23. These traits extend to money. **God expects us to be like Him when it comes to money.**

In this section, we will look at how to become "godly" in financial matters. We take a look at some very basic financial and economic concepts used in the Kingdom of Israel and the Kingdom of Heaven, and look to see how they can be applied to the lives of today's Believers. The objective is not to make you a financial wizard, a home-schooled CPA, CFA, economist, or to turn your personal finances around overnight, but to share some very basic insights into the interconnectivity of finance, economics and Kingdom living.

Nations that fail to implement strong economic principles are playing Russian roulette with their citizens. Usually such games do not end well. Many marriages fail because of poor financial management. Many persons underachieve in their lives because they didn't learn how to manage money. Even the world teaches people how to make money, but few teach people how to manage it. Managing money is actually more important to Believers than it is to non-Believers for three reasons, God, tithes and offering. These are not things that non-Believers have to consider in their financial plans, but they are very important to Believers.

God wants us to be good stewards, and I believe this includes money. Read on and let's explore how.

Chapter 7

Kingdom Macroeconomics (Financial Morality)

God's macroeconomic plan was meticulously developed over time. He designed it personally. You will not find His plan in an economic or financial textbook. It's even difficult to find His plan in the Bible, but it's there, hidden like most spiritual things. In order to uncover His economic plan, first, we will delve into the economic plan that was established by Moses for the children of Israel. In a feeble attempt to be creative, we called Moses' economic plan "Mosenomics." I know...not very creative, huh? I promise not to quit my day job. Putting the name aside, understanding the principles of Mosenomics is very important because they laid the foundation of God's ultimate economic plan for this Era of God's Kingdom.

Mosenomics

Moses was trained as a high-ranking official in Egypt and was well-studied in the things of the Egyptian kingdom (see Acts 7:22). His training undoubtedly included economics. The Egyptians historically seemed to manage their financial and economic affairs better than many of their neighbouring countries. Ancient Egypt was a blessed country, being well-positioned near the River Nile. They took advantage of the natural resources to advance trade and agriculture. When many countries in the neighbouring desert regions suffered mercilessly under droughts, Egypt used its highly developed irrigation systems and its expert knowledge on the ebb and flow of the Nile to maintain a healthy supply of marketable crops. We know of at least two biblical legends, Abraham and Jacob, who were forced to use the resources of Egypt to sustain themselves during major famines in their days. Despite some of the notoriety it gained in Christendom, due in large part to what happened between Pharaoh and Moses, God used Egypt to bless His people multiple times.

Genesis 12:10 (KJV) And there was a famine in the land: and Abram went down into Egypt to sojourn there; for the famine was grievous in the land.

Genesis 42:1-2 (KJV) Now when Jacob saw that there was corn in Egypt, Jacob said unto his sons, Why do ye look one upon another? ²And he said, Behold, I have heard that there is corn in Egypt: get you down thither, and buy for us from thence; that we may live, and not die.

Even our Lord Jesus, as a young child, was sent to Egypt for protection against Herod.

Matthew 2:13 (KJV) And when they were departed, behold, the angel of the Lord appeareth to Joseph in a dream, saying, Arise, and take the young child and his mother, and flee into Egypt, and be thou there until I bring thee word: for Herod will seek the young child to destroy him.

It is believed that the Egyptian economy was booming during the days of Moses, no doubt in significant part due to the forced labour of the Hebrews. In Egypt, the state owned the land, and its King (Pharaoh) controlled everything. He dictated the compensation and taxation of the people, who effectively worked for him. Social status meant everything in Egypt, and the people were very divided. At that time, the Hebrews were enslaved by the Egyptians. Although a Hebrew, Moses was adopted by Pharaoh's daughter and therefore was included among the elites in the land. Because of this, Moses was a free man, and he was wealthy. In Egypt, the Pharaoh ruled the entire nation. He had a second in command, whom they called Vizier, who supervised the administration of the entire government apparatus. You will recall the story of Joseph, Jacob's son, who was sold by his brothers but eventually became a Vizier in Egypt.

Moses obviously benefited from his experience in Egypt. He became a close friend of God. These gave him a unique vantage point on the topic of economics and finance. We can find Moses' economic philosophies in Deuteronomy (chapter 14:22 through chapter 15). It should be of no surprise that he designed the Hebrew economy to be driven by agriculture and farming. This is what they did in Egypt.

In Moses' kingdom government, God would be its "Pharaoh," and Moses himself acted as its Vizier. The Priests and Levites would serve as the spiritual arm of the kingdom, and they would be dedicated to God. This is similar to what Moses experienced in Egypt, where the priests had become somewhat autonomous and developed a system of oracles whereby, they were the voice of their gods on matters requiring spiritual counsel. Israel's priests would not own land and would not work regular jobs but serve as religious guides for the people of God. They would be paid through the tithes (10%) from the other Hebrews. Because of this, the priests were not self-sufficient. Moses built a system whereby they relied on everyone else for support. In this way, keeping everyone spiritually fit and balanced served to protect their own interests as priests because they all relied on God to provide for them.

Moses believed in a strong welfare system. This is where Moses departed from Egyptian philosophies. The Egyptians were keen to keep the social and economic classes as they were. The rich would stay rich and the poor, "who cared?" That seemed to be their attitude. Well, Moses cared, and because of it, he designed a system that he felt would better serve "the people." Moses had high hopes to drive poverty out of Israel (Deuteronomy 15:4), and his economic philosophy centred around this concept. Below are some of his aggressive social programs:

- He instituted a special tithe for the poor and strangers (Deuteronomy 14:28-29). This was over and above the annual tithes.

- He established a release program for protecting Hebrew borrowers. Each seventh year, lenders in the economy would be required to write off the debt of borrowers. (Deuteronomy 15:1-3)

- Moses made it mandatory for wealthy Hebrews to lend to the poor. (Deuteronomy 15:7-8)

- Granting loans would be mandatory even if the request was close to the release year noted above (for example, year six). (Deuteronomy 15:9-10)

- Hebrew slave masters could only contract Hebrew slaves for six years. It was mandatory to offer them freedom in the seventh year. (Deuteronomy 15:12)

- In such cases, the master had to give gifts liberally to the freed slaves from their possessions. (Deuteronomy 15:13-14)

At the heart of Mosenomics was the fact that Israel, **as a nation**, would be blessed by God as long as they kept God's commandments. This is how Israel would build its national income, or GDP (Gross Domestic Product). The nation would follow God, and God would bless them. God would also make them an economic powerhouse compared to other countries. They would be a lender to other nations, and would not have to borrow from others. Deuteronomy 15:5-6 (KJV) states:

> *⁵Only if thou carefully hearken unto the voice of the Lord thy God, to observe to do all these commandments which I command thee this day. ⁶For the Lord thy God blesseth thee, as he promised thee: and **thou shalt lend unto many nations**, but thou shalt not borrow; and **thou shalt reign over many nations**, but they shall not reign over thee.*

Many people have personalized this scripture. They appeared to have concluded that God was referring to individuals when He said "thou" will lend, and "thou" will reign, apparently making the connection that this promise meant that they, as an individual, would be a lender to or would reign over many nations. However, it seems unlikely that God meant that individuals will reign over nations. God appears to be referring to the nation of Israel when He proclaimed this blessing.

Deuteronomy 28:13 is also often interpreted this way. Still, that scripture seems better aligned with the concept that the nation of Israel, as opposed to individual people within the nation, would be the head and not the tail, etc. Actually, the blessings and curses of Deuteronomy 28 appear to be specifically addressed to the nation of Israel. In verse 1, the Bible specifically states, "the Lord thy God will set thee on high above all nations of the earth." He definitely did not intend to set every individual within Israel above every other nation on earth. He must have meant the nation of Israel. Verse 9 is more direct. God said, "The Lord will establish you as his own, **a holy nation**" (CEB).

Frankly, within Israel, some persons were expected to benefit more from the economy than others. Despite the overwhelming blessings as a nation, not everyone would become wealthy. Some were expected to remain poor. As a nation, Israel would be a lender and not a borrower. Within Israel, some persons would be lenders, while others would be borrowers. Some would be masters, and other Hebrews would serve them as slaves. Here are a few comments that Moses made in this regard, which prove the point:

> *Deuteronomy 15:11-12 (KJV)* ¹¹ ***For the poor shall never cease out of the land:*** *therefore I command thee, saying, Thou shalt open thine hand wide **unto thy brother, to thy poor, and to thy needy**, in thy land.* ¹² ***And if thy brother, an***

Hebrew man, or an Hebrew woman, be sold unto thee, *and serve thee six years; then in the seventh year thou shalt let him go free from thee.*

When people promote the concept that every Christian will be the head and not the tail, etc., they are promoting a false narrative and peddling false hope to God's people. It might seem innocent enough; it might even appear to motivate God's people to have greater faith in the possibilities and power of God, but there are some unintended negative impacts that should be considered. First, this type of message promotes the exultation of self and greed. Jesus preached the exact opposite. He said that the greatest in His kingdom is the one who is the servant (or least). We spent a lot of time in This Book addressing the image of God and what it means. This kind of message is contradictory to God's image. Second, this kind of message eventually engenders doubt and disbelief in many persons. Undoubtedly, some persons, albeit a few, will arise from such messages to achieve great things in the future. However, most will not. I contend that it is those individuals who will eventually become frustrated, question God, and lose focus on the true gospel of Jesus Christ. While looking for those blessings, they lose sight of God.

Moses understood the difference between the macro and the microeconomic landscapes within Israel, which is what drove him to develop the programs that we noted above. If Moses expected every Hebrew to be wealthy, or even to be able to take care of themselves, there would be no need for such dramatic wealth redistribution policies that Moses established.

The redistribution programs not only provided for economic opportunities for the poor, but they also provided for the protection of the poor from being taken advantage of. In Deuteronomy 15:9-10, Moses instructed the wealthy Hebrews not to turn down the poor and needy for purely economic reasons.

Deuteronomy 15:9-10 (KJV) *⁹ Beware that there be not a thought in thy wicked heart, saying, The seventh year, the year of release, is at hand; and thine eye be evil against thy poor brother, and thou givest him nought; and he cry unto the Lord against thee,* ***and it be sin unto thee***. *¹⁰ Thou shalt surely give him, and thine heart shall not be grieved when thou givest unto him:* ***because*** *that for this thing the Lord thy God shall bless thee in all thy works, and in all that thou puttest thine hand unto.*

Moses deemed it a sin for persons to withhold assistance from the poor. He was very clear about it—they must help the poor! In verse 10, Moses also wanted to make sure that persons did not demean the poor when they assisted them. He commanded the wealthy that when helping the poor, they must not act "off," but instead, they must do it with a pleasant disposition. That's what he meant by "and thine heart shall not be grieved when thou <u>givest</u>." Paul reinforced this principle when he wrote, "God loveth a cheerful giver" in 2 Corinthians 9:7. He said something similar in Romans 12:8 "he that giveth, let him do it with simplicity."

The second important point Moses commanded in Deuteronomy 15:10 related to the reason why it was important that the wealthy give generously and cheerfully to the poor. He said that the Lord will bless them because of it. However, God's blessings start before then because He would have already blessed them with wealth to enable them to have something to give. One might argue that because they have already been blessed financially, when the wealthy give to the poor, it is more about them giving to prevent their blessings from being stopped rather than for them to be blessed. Put another way, the benefit of giving is for God's persistent or ongoing blessings.

On the flip side, although he wanted to help the poor, Moses nevertheless did not envision the poor taking advantage of the rich. He felt that the poor would have ample protection in the Laws, and therefore they had no need to be dishonest and manipulative. Moses, therefore, offered some defense for lenders, by tying the amount that they would give to the amount that the poor actually needed, as opposed to the amount that they wanted. This is gleaned from verse 8 of Deuteronomy 15 below:

*Deuteronomy 15:8 (KJV) But thou shalt open thine hand wide unto him, and shalt surely lend him **sufficient for his need**, in that which he wanteth.*

In this statement, Moses simultaneously ensured that the rich do not skimp on their support to the poor, while preventing the poor from abusing the rich.

The following diagram depicts Israel's national economic plan.

Jesunomics

Jesus also spoke about economics. Frankly, He spoke about it a lot. In the 37 parables that He told, Jesus spoke about economics in at least 50% of them. Let's remember that economics deals with money, wealth, poverty (types of welfare), employment, productivity, industries, and many other topics. Economics was very important in His day, and clearly, it was important to Him to deliver messages to us. The only topic Jesus covered more than economics is the topic of the Kingdom, but that's because economics is a subtopic of the Kingdom. In that way, they are inextricably bound to one another.

During His sermon on the Kingdom (Sermon on The Mount), Jesus shared some very important titbits about His Kingdom philosophies on finance and economics. Chapter 6 of Matthew elaborates on some of His economic vision for the people of God. While Moses attempted to redistribute income so that everyone was financially secure in their promised land, Jesus instead focused on His promised land, Heaven. Therefore, His economic focus was on how His people are to build their fortunes in the kingdom of Heaven. In the Kingdom Sermon on the Mount, Jesus said this:

Matthew 6:19-21 (KJV) *¹⁹ **Lay not up for yourselves treasures upon earth**, where moth and rust doth corrupt, and where thieves break through and steal: ²⁰ **But lay up for yourselves treasures in heaven**, where neither moth nor rust doth corrupt, and* *where thieves do not break through nor steal: ²¹For where your treasure is, there will your heart be also.*

This was an economic statement from Jesus about wealth. He admonished us to lay treasures up in Heaven. It turns out that **Jesus regularly preached and taught about Heaven as a means to motivate His disciples**. Below are a few examples (text in curly brackets added). When reading them, try to focus on His tone. His tone was more than to instruct; it was to motivate.

*John 14:1-3 (KJV) Let not your hearts be troubled {**Don't be discouraged**}: ye believe in God, believe also in me. ²In my Father's house are many mansions {**I have an abundance for you**}: if it were not so, I would have told you {**You can trust me**}. I go to prepare a place for you {**I'm looking out for you**}. ³And if I go and prepare a place for you, I will come again {**I promise**}, and receive you unto myself; that where I am, there ye may be also {**You will live in paradise with me**}*

*Luke 6:20 (KJV) And he lifted up his eyes on his disciples, and said, Blessed be ye poor: for yours is the kingdom of God {**I will take care of the poor. I promise to bless you**}.*

John 16:16-18, 20, 22 (KJV) ¹⁶A little while, and ye shall not see me: and again, a little while, and ye shall see me, because I go to the Father. ¹⁷Then said some of his disciples among themselves, What is this that he saith unto us, A little while, and ye shall not see me: and again, a little while, and ye shall see me: and, because I go to the Father? ¹⁸They said, therefore, What is this that he saith, A little while? we cannot tell what he saith.

*²⁰Verily, verily, I say unto you, That ye shall weep and lament, but the world shall rejoice: and ye shall be sorrowful, but your sorrow shall be turned into joy. {**Stick with me. You will be rewarded**}*

*²²And ye now therefore have sorrow: but I will see you again, and your heart shall rejoice, and your joy no man taketh from you. {**In the end, you will win. Just wait until I come back**}*

Jesus wanted us to be focused on Heaven! This included our financial focus. He wanted us to focus on building "wealth" in Heaven rather than focusing on earth. He said that we cannot serve God and mammon (Matthew 6:24). To those of us who are working hard building wealth on earth, Jesus instead wants us to use that same focus and energy on the accumulation of spiritual treasures; things of His Kingdom. A person may ask, how do we lay up treasures in Heaven? One answer is found in the following scripture:

> *Mark 10:21 (KJV) Then Jesus beholding him loved him, and said unto him, One thing thou lackest: go thy way, sell whatsoever thou hast, and **give to the poor, and thou shalt have treasure in heaven**: and come, take up the cross, and follow me.*

One way to lay treasures in Heaven is to give to the poor. In the single statement that Jesus gave about wealth (that we should lay it up in Heaven), it seems probable that He may have been making a hidden, yet equally potent statement, that we are to give to the poor. It is indisputable that Jesus consistently taught us to help the poor. It's because this is important to Him, and it should also be important to us. Here is another example of Jesus promoting His desire to help the poor:

> *Luke 14:12-14 (KJV) [12] Then said he also to him that bade him, When thou makest a dinner or a supper, call not thy friends, nor thy brethren, neither thy kinsmen, nor thy rich neighbours; lest they also bid thee again, and a recompence be made thee. [13] **But when thou makest a feast, call the poor, the maimed, the lame, the blind:** [14] **And thou shalt be blessed**; for they cannot recompense thee: **for thou shalt be recompensed at the resurrection of the just.***

What challenging, yet transparent words from Jesus! Instead of inviting our friends and rich neighbours, He wants us to invite the poor, the maimed, the lame and the blind. Of course, this list is not exhaustive. It's more of a guide to help us know who He wants us to assist. In addition to this, He is saying to us that we should not pursue strategies that will result in worldly rewards. From a carnal perspective, it seems wise to invite people to my house party who can help me, like rich neighbours, politicians, business leaders, and such. Who knows how God will use them to bless me later. But, like Paul said, the carnal mind is enmity against God (Romans 8:7). The flesh (our human nature) cannot please God (Romans 8:8).

Notice, also, in Luke 14:14, the focus on being rewarded in Heaven. That's where we are to look for our rewards. That's where our hope lies, and it should be where our focus remains.

Jesus, like Moses, commanded us to lend to anyone who would borrow from us (Matthew 5:42). Both of them, therefore, believed in an absolute responsibility of the rich to help the poor. Like Moses, Jesus wanted to make certain that our attitude was right. Therefore, He said that when we do almsgiving, we must do it in secret, being confident that our Father, who sees in secret, will reward us openly. The reward is attached to the gift **and** the intention behind the gift. Doing it secretly means that we have no ulterior motive. On the other hand, Jesus indicated that those who promote their giving "have their reward."

The reward that Jesus spoke about in the above scripture will be awarded in Heaven. After all, Jesus commanded that we are to lay treasures in Heaven and not on earth. However, there are other scriptures that support this conclusion.

Jesus gave another example of how treasures can be laid up in Heaven in the Gospel of Luke:

Luke 6:22-23 (KJV) [22]Blessed are ye, when men shall hate you, and when they shall separate you from their company, and shall reproach you, and cast out your name as evil, for the Son of man's sake. [23]Rejoice ye in that day, and leap for joy: **for, behold, your reward is great in heaven***: for in the like manner did their fathers unto the prophets.*

A third scripture, which seems to wrap this discussion up well, is found in Revelation 22, which is the last book of the Bible, and among the last words attributed to Jesus.

Revelation 22:12 (KJV) And, behold, I come quickly; and my reward is with me, to give every man according as his work shall be.

The Lord's Prayer about Finances

Just like Moses, Jesus taught that God would be our provider. He affirmed this in the Lord's prayer. In the Lord's prayer, Jesus taught us how to pray about finances. He talked about daily bread and debt; "Give us this day our daily bread. And forgive us our debt, as we forgive our debtors" (Matthew 6:11-12). First of all, as this prayer is to God, Jesus wanted His disciples to know who their source of financial blessings is. It is "Our Father, which art in Heaven" (Matthew 6:9). God is our source!

But what did Jesus mean by "daily bread" in this prayer? What was He referencing? His teaching about daily bread seemed to have been derived from the experience that Israel had with manna in the wilderness. In the book of Exodus (chapter 16), after the children of Israel left Egypt, God led them into the wilderness, but they did not have sufficient food or water to sustain them on their journey. God provided food for them by way of bread (manna), which fell from Heaven.

> *Exodus 16:4-5 (KJV)* *⁴Then said the Lord unto Moses, Behold,* ***I will rain bread*** ***from heaven for you;*** *and the people shall go out* ***and gather a certain rate every*** ***day,*** *that I may prove them, whether they will walk in my law, or no. ⁵And it shall come to pass, that on the sixth day they shall prepare that which they bring in; and it shall be twice as much as they gather daily.*

God was their provider, just as Jesus is teaching us that He is and will be our provider. But God gave them specific instructions that they were to gather a certain amount daily for five days, and on the sixth day (the day before Sabbath), they would gather exactly double the amount because manna would not fall on the Sabbath.

Everyone was allowed to gather manna according to their specific situation. More specifically, they could gather based on the number of their "persons." This means that some families got more, and some got less. Everyone would not gather up the same amount.

> *Exodus 16:16-17 (KJV)* *¹⁶This is the thing which the Lord hath commanded, Gather of it every man according to his eating, an omer for every man,* ***according to*** ***the number of your persons;*** *take ye every man for them which are in his tents.* *¹⁷* ***And the children of Israel did so, and gathered, some more, some less.***

If manna were money today, it means that everyone would not make the same amount; however, we would make sufficient for the number of our "persons." Persons represent individuals whom God has placed in our care. This definitely means family, but it probably means more. It means that God blesses us to take care of persons in our surroundings who need help.

Concerning the first five days, they were instructed not to allow the bread to be stored until the next day (verse 19). He didn't want them to keep it because He would provide more for them the next day. He wanted to test ("prove") their faith in Him. As expected, the Hebrews did not heed to this, but instead, they saved some for the next day. Honestly, I can easily see myself doing the same thing. If money dropped from Heaven every day, I would get bags, hire workers, and buy buildings to store up the money, and let's face it, so would you. It's what we do instinctively. We are drawn to success and wealth. Normal people don't just choose poverty and failure for themselves, especially when they don't have much money, to begin with. And the children of Israel were no different.

It turned out, however, that when they tried to save the bread and kept some overnight, it rotted by the next morning and stank (verse 20). But on the sixth day, when they gathered double as God commanded, the extra that they gathered and kept overnight did not rot or stink on the Sabbath day.

Interestingly, though the people had bread for the Sabbath day, some still went out on the Sabbath day looking for more. Either because of greed (wanting more than their portions) or indiscipline (failure to budget), they went back; but no manna fell on the Sabbath because God only intended for them to have sufficient bread for each day–their daily bread, as it were.

This story is emblematic of our human greed. We are driven, most of us, to grow, build, succeed, but we often take more than what is needed. Bread was like money to them, and they wanted to store up as much as they could. They wanted wealth. They wanted to take care of their families. They wanted to secure their futures. These are concepts that any good financial planner would advise her clients. But counterintuitively, these were not what God instructed them to do.

In Matthew 6:34, Jesus said, "Sufficient for the day is the evil thereof." Jesus was talking about money, and he concluded his talk by admonishing us to seek His Kingdom before we seek wealth, food, clothing, shelter, because our heavenly Father knows that we have need of these things. He brought us back to the manna experience, and He is teaching us today that we ought only to pursue our daily bread, but when God blesses us with more, we are to share the excess.

Early Church Economics

There are a few stories in Acts that encapsulate Jesunomics, suggesting that the Apostles followed it.

Acts 4:32-37 (KJV) *[32]And the multitude of them that believed were of one heart and of one soul: neither said any of them that ought of the things which he possessed was his own; but they had all things common. [33]And with great power gave the apostles witness of the resurrection of the Lord Jesus: and great grace was upon them all.* ***[34]Neither was there any among them that lacked: for as many as were possessors of lands or houses sold them, and brought the prices of the things that were sold, [35]And laid them down at the apostles' feet: and distribution was*** *made unto every man according as he had need.* *36And Joses, who by the apostles was surnamed Barnabas, (which is, being interpreted, The son of consolation,) a Levite, and of the country of Cyprus, 37Having land, sold it, and brought the money, and laid it at the apostles' feet.*

While Acts 4 may be the more popular example of how early Christians responded to Jesus' teachings about economics, it was not the first. An earlier reference was made in Acts 2 after the disciples were first filled with the Holy Spirit. The Bible reveals in verses 44 and 45:

Acts 2:44-46 (KJV) 44And all that believed were together, and had all things common; 45And sold their possessions and goods, and parted them to all men, as every man had need.

The Apostles demonstrated the meaning of "your persons" (see Exodus 16:16) by going beyond their immediate family. To them, this concept was communal. These Apostles were trained directly by Jesus, and this is how they interpreted His teachings about finances and economics. The daily bread (money in this case) was earned by individuals who used their affluence to contribute to the building of the community so that no one lacked.

God established the Kingdom principles regarding economics, and we have done everything in our power to walk back from His ways. But we weren't the first. Ananias and Sapphire did the same thing and paid the ultimate price for it. They are a warning for us, and as the old adage goes, "A word to the wise is sufficient."

The Kingdom policy on economics requires us to be united as they were in the early church. It also requires us to understand that God expects us to help the poor. This is the responsibility of the rich just as much as it is the responsibility of the church. In these scriptures in Acts, the common threads were that they were united and that one of the common goals was to ensure that everyone's needs were satisfied, with the assistance of everyone else who prospered.

God blesses some of us specifically, so we can, in turn, provide for others. God always expected us to give to one another, but we have become obsessed with receiving from God, and because of this, we are no longer able to see God's intent nor His image. Remember, it is God's intent that we are inward out focused, which means that we must help others.

Another scripture that we all know, that bears witness to Jesus' Kingdom principle, is found in Acts 20. We are also reminded that by the word of two or three witnesses, shall every word be established (2 Corinthians 13:1). This is the third scriptural reference to this precise Kingdom concept.

*Acts 20:35 (KJV) I have shewed you all things, how that so labouring **ye ought to support the weak**, and to remember the words of the Lord Jesus, how he said, **It is more blessed to give than to receive**.*

Jesus' economic plan is shown in the following diagram:

What's a dollar worth?

To those persons who believe that we are to be rewarded financially when we give money away, I have a question for you. How much is $1 worth in the kingdom? In other words, if we give $1 in our church offering pan (or to the poor), how much is it worth in kingdom blessings? Put yet another way, are we to be rewarded financially based on the value of our gift? I would say no, resoundingly, because if we are rewarded based on the value of our gift, then it stands to reason that the persons who gives the most will be rewarded the most. That logic would mean that a person who gives $10 will be rewarded less than the person who gives $100. Most people might not have any disagreement with this. That's how it works on earth. But is it how it works in Heaven? Let's see.

Continuing with this assumption, that we are rewarded in Heaven based on the value of the money we give, it would, therefore, mean that the person who has more to give has an advantage when it comes to the amount of the reward that they are eligible to receive, if in fact we are to be blessed based on the dollar value of our gift. This would be most unfair to poor people, wouldn't it? Yes, it would! And it would make God extremely partial to the rich, which we know He is not. This, therefore, raises a major question about how we would monetize (or value) our giving. Since God does not favour the rich, how does He fairly quantify the value of our love offerings? What is our offering really worth, if $10 on earth is not worth $10 in heaven? Jesus gave us the answer to this question in the following scripture:

Luke 21:1-4 (KJV) And he looked up, and saw the rich men casting their gifts into the treasury. ²And he saw also a certain poor widow casting in thither two mites. ³And he said, Of a truth I say unto you, that this poor widow hath cast in more than they all: ⁴For all these have of their abundance cast in unto the offerings of God: but she of her penury hath cast in all the living that she had.

So then, giving out of our abundance is not valued as highly as giving out of our poverty. To explain, let's consider two economic concepts of inflation and deflation. Inflation occurs when the purchasing power of money decreases. This means that when inflation occurs, because prices rise, we cannot purchase the same amount of goods or services with the amount of money that we paid in the past. As an example, if there is a 1% inflation, it means that certain products that we paid $100 for in the past would now cost $101 after inflation. Deflation, on the other hand, occurs when the purchasing power of money today is worth more than in the past. Using a similar example, a 1% deflation means that the same items that we paid $100 for in the past will now cost us $99.

This analogy, while imperfect, gets the point across. To elaborate, we need to define the difference between the gifts of the rich men and that of the widow. The rich men, according to Jesus, gave out of their abundance. This means that after they gave, their residual wealth was not significantly affected. They still had a lot of money left. The widow, on the other hand, gave out of her penury. This means that after she gave, her residual wealth was materially affected. She didn't have much wealth before she gave, and afterward, she had nothing left because she "cast in all the living that she had."

Based on this distinction, when we give comfortably out of our abundance of wealth, it's as if the price of our reward has inflated, making our gift less valuable. It's not worth as much as the nominal value of the monies that we give. In other words, if a rich person puts $100 in the offering pan, it's purchasing power is not worth $100 in Heaven, figuratively speaking. But when we give out of our lack, as the widow did, the price of our rewards in Heaven deflate, thereby allowing us to purchase more heavenly rewards for the monetary value of the gift. As Jesus said, the widow's two earthly pennies that she gave were worth more in Heaven than all of the offerings that the rich people gave. **Therefore, in the Kingdom of God, the little that we give here on earth, when it is given out of our lack, is translated into more when determining the level of our reward in Heaven.**

This reminds me of an incident in the old testament that befuddled me for years. It's the story of the widow from Zarephath who gave the prophet Elijah her last meal. As the Bible tells it, Elijah had earlier prophesied that there would be a famine in the land, and it happened. It was really severe. At first, God sent Elijah to the brook of Cherith, near Jordan, where he would have the water from the brook to drink, and where he would be fed by ravens. After a while, the brook dried up because of the famine; then, God sent Elijah to the gentile widow from Zarephath to get sustenance.

Elijah asked the widow for water and bread. She told him that she and her son only had a handful of bread left to eat. The prophet responded to her this way:

> *1 Kings 17:13-14 (KJV) ¹³And Elijah said unto her, Fear not; go and do as thou hast said: **but make me thereof a little cake first**, and bring it unto me, and after make for thee and for thy son. ¹⁴For thus saith the Lord God of Israel, The barrel of meal shall not waste, neither shall the cruse of oil fail, until the day that the Lord sendeth rain upon the earth.*

This used to bother me, that Elijah asked her to feed him first, even before her son. But that was before I saw how this experience symbolized the importance of putting God ahead of food, shelter, and clothing as per Matthew 6:33.

Sowing Seed

I know what most of you are probably thinking. This completely upsets the applecart when it comes to sowing seed and the returns that we have been taught to expect from it. We very often hear that we should sow seed, and we will be rewarded 100-fold. However, this concept assumes that the reward is tied to the monetary value of the gift (i.e., the cash value). That if you give, for example, $100, you will be rewarded 100%, which is $100 for a net reward of $200. In the last section, we completely debunked that concept. However, some may not be convinced, so let's dig deeper.

The reference to 100-fold blessing also assumes that when Jesus spoke about being rewarded 30, 60, and 100-fold, He was referring to giving. **He was not!** Instead, the seed that He was referring to was part of His explanation of how the Word of God, when planted into good ground, yields fruit/reward (Mark 4:3-8). It's the Word of God that will yield fruit, not giving money. Some may disregard this argument by saying that this was only a parable, but my response is that one may take some liberty in interpreting other parables, but not this one. Jesus gave us the interpretation for this one, thus leaving no room for personal revelations.

The other time Jesus spoke about 100-fold reward was when He told His disciples that anyone who leaves their houses, mother, wife, children, etc. for His sake would receive 100-fold "in this time" and also eternal life (Mark 10:30). Firstly, Jesus was not speaking about money. The Disciples mentioned to Him that they **left everything** to follow Him, and this was His reply to them about leaving everything. He didn't mention money. Secondly, He was not speaking literally about the rewards. Even if one were inclined to hope that He was speaking literally about houses or lands, they would have to question how one would **literally** receive 100-fold more mothers, or fathers, or wives, in return. Thirdly, one would have to justify what Jesus meant by adding "with persecutions" as part of the return. Fourthly, it is illogical to give up things for Jesus, only to receive 100 times more of the same things given up. For the reasons above, it is clear that Jesus was not using this as a lesson about being rewarded for sowing seed.

There is another scripture in Genesis 26:12, which talks about how Isaac sowed, and reaped 100-fold that year. It's undeniable that God blessed Isaac tremendously, even in the midst of the famine. The scripture bears witness to this. But was it really because He sowed seed? You might imagine that my answer is no. The problem with blessings is sometimes it's a chicken or egg thing. Sometimes people mistake God's blessings with their wisdom and talents. What do I mean? In verses 2 and 3, the Bible tells us that God appeared to Isaac and told him to go to a specific place where he would be blessed despite being in the famine. God promised the blessing **before** Isaac sowed a single seed. He did this to make sure that all of us know and understand that it was not the sowing of the seed that resulted in the great harvest, but the harvest was received because God promised to bless him. The blessing came because he followed God's instructions and went where he was told to go. Therefore, as with everything else in God, it came by faith, not by works.

We noted earlier that God blesses some persons more than others. That's part of His design. Consider Jacob, Isaac's son. There was a famine in the land during Jacob's time, just as there was during Isaac's. Because of God's divine plan, He sent Jacob to Egypt, whereas did specifically told Isaac not to go to Egypt (Genesis 26:2). God already had a plan for Israel (Jacob) to go Egypt and to eventually suffer oppression at the hand of the Egyptians.

Also, note that Jacob didn't reap the same level of rewards as Isaac. However, God made it clear that Jacob was no less called or anointed than his father Isaac because God called Himself the God of Abraham, Isaac, and Jacob. Jacob did not receive the same blessings in his famine as Isaac did, but God did not minimize Jacob's place. He is still the God of Jacob. In fact, the nation of Israel is actually named after Jacob, not Isaac.

Finally, let's consider another scripture about sowing seed. Paul said:

*Galatians 6:7-10 (KJV) [7]Be not deceived; God is not mocked: for whatsoever a man soweth, that shall he also reap. [8]For **he that soweth to his flesh shall of the flesh reap corruption; but he that soweth to the Spirit shall of the Spirit reap life everlasting.** [9]And let us not be weary in well doing: for in due season we shall reap, if we faint not. [10]As we have therefore opportunity, let us do good unto all men, especially unto them who are of the household of faith.*

Although verse 7 says that we will reap what we sow, this is often misinterpreted. I have heard many teach that this means that the thing which I sow is the same as what I will reap, literally. Examples used to justify this conclusion are fruit; for example, when you sow grape seeds, you will reap grape trees and hence grapes. By extension, they teach that in order to reap money, we have to sow money. This is not what Paul was saying. He explained himself very thoroughly. He said that when we sow to our flesh, we will reap corruption from the flesh, and when we sow to the Holy Spirit, we will reap everlasting life from the Holy Spirit. The thing sowed to the flesh is not corruption, nor is the thing sowed to the Spirit everlasting life, yet, these are the things that we reap. Interestingly, money is only useful in this life, that is, to the flesh. Those of us who are money-seekers should consider this scripture. When we seek and store wealth in abundance, we are sowing to our flesh. Sowing to the flesh leads to corruption (or death).

It's really easy to justify ourselves by taking scriptures out of context. The litmus test should be that before we conclude on any interpretation, we should see how it lines up with the rest of the Bible. If there are multiple other scriptures that bring into question what you propose, or if something you believe is contrary to what Jesus expressly taught, you may be on shaky ground. Remember that Satan has mastered the art of misdirection and misinterpretation when it comes to the scriptures, and he usually gets us to bite the hook when it's loaded with bait; things that satisfy our flesh, like money, wealth and success.

PERSONAL APPLICATION
DOOR # 2

In Matthew 6:1-18, Jesus talked about rewards. He used three different experiences in which we may be rewarded, 1) Almsgiving; 2) Prayer; and 3) Fasting. In each case, Jesus basically talked about two scenarios with different results; lets call them Door #1 and Door #2.

Behind Door #1 is the reward for persons who publicize their almsgiving, prayer and fasting. Door #2 hides the reward for persons who do these things in secret. In all three cases, Jesus commands that we do them in secret in order to be rewarded by our heavenly Father. When we do them publicly, Jesus insinuates that we will not be rewarded by our Father. This appears clear enough.

However, there is something else interesting about these passages. Jesus used two different words which were interpreted as reward. Each time He talked about the Father rewarding us, He used the Greek word Apodidomi. He used it three times; Matthew 4, 6 and 18. All other times, He used the Greek word Misthos.

Strong's Concordance defines Misthos as "wages, hire", while it defines Apodidomi as "to give up, give back, return, restore." In the case of Misthos, something is being earned, while in the case of Apodidomi, something is being given up.

This distinction is too blatant to be a mistake. The fact that He did it three times consecutively means that He had a specific reason for doing it.

What, then, is the meaning behind this? It appears that Jesus is making a distinction that coincides with His Parable of the Labourers in the Vineyard found in Matthew 20:1-16. In this parable, Jesus described the Kingdom as a landowner who went out early in the morning to hire workers for the vineyard. He hired another set of persons at 9 am, noon, 3 pm, and 5 pm. At the end of the workday, the landowner paid all of them the same amount. This bothered the persons who worked for the entire day because they worked longer than the others and expected to receive more. The landowner rejected this notion, indicating that it is his option to pay the other persons as much as he chose. He also called their complaint evil.

Jesus wants us to understand that what we will be given (rewarded) from our Father is something that is not earned, but is gifted by Him to us. The reward is a gift, not a repayment. The Bible says that the wages of sin is death, but the gift of God is eternal life (Romans 6:23). Gifts are not earned; they are given. Any reward that we get from God is not earned. It is a gift from God.

There is another example in the Bible when Jesus used these two words (Apodidomi and Misthos) in the same thought. It is found in Revelation 22:12.

> *12And, behold, I come quickly; and my reward is with me, to give every man according as his work shall be.*

The word "reward" in this text is Misthos and the word "give" is Apodidomi. However, this time the translation for Apodidomi is different. It is translated as give, but this time He ties the gift to work. Even though He is gifting us something, it is based on the lives that we live. The preceding verse from Revelation 22:11 helps us with this.

> *11He that is unjust, let him be unjust still: and he which is filthy, let him be filthy still: and he that is righteous, let him be righteous still: and he that is holy, let him be holy still.*

So then, the reward is not a payment but a gift.

You may now be asking, "What is the gift?." Before I respond, I want to point out another observation. It is that the word reward is often interpreted in singular form when referring to what we receive from God. This suggests a specific gift is being referenced. Continuing with verse 13 and 14 of Revelation 22, we see that the gift is heaven and all that it entails.

> *13I am Alpha and Omega, the beginning and the end, the first and the last. 14Blessed are they that do his commandments, that they may have right to the tree of life, and may enter in through the gates into the city.*

The gift from our Father is access to heaven, the city prepared for all who love God and keep His commandments. This is our ultimate reward and it's the same reward for us all. It is the beautiful heaven described in Revelation 21. This is what is behind Door #2. Those who keep His commandments get this gift. Everyone else will get what is behind Door #1. Jesus described this as weeping and gnashing of teeth (Matthew 13:50). I definitely want the Father's gift, which is behind Door #2. This means that even though I cannot earn it, there are still things that I must do to be gifted it. First, I must believe in Jesus; second, repent/turn from sinful ways; third, be baptised in water and the Spirit; fourth, keep His commandments.

Patrick James McFall

Chapter 8

Kingdom Wealth (Role of the Rich)

To have, or not to have

There are some of us who think that financial sacrifice is akin to godliness. The more we suffer for Christ, including financially (i.e., poverty), the more we please God. To them, money is nothing more than a commodity or tool to be used. They see the dark side of money and are cautious of its potentially harmful effects. There are, actually, some scriptures that appear, at least at some level, to support this point of view. Here are a few:

1 Timothy 6:10 (KJV) For the love of money is the root of all evil: which while some coveted after, they have erred from the faith, and pierced themselves through with many sorrows.

Matthew 6:24 (KJV) No man can serve two masters: for either he will hate the one, and love the other; or else he will hold to the one, and despise the other. Ye cannot serve God and mammon.

Matthew 6:34 (KJV) Take therefore no thought for the morrow: for the morrow shall take thought for the things of itself. Sufficient unto the day is the evil thereof.

Hebrews 13:5 (KJV) Let your conversation be without covetousness; and be content with such things as ye have: for he hath said, I will never leave thee, nor forsake thee.

Luke 12:15 (KJV) And he said unto them, Take heed, and beware of covetousness: for a man's life consisteth not in the abundance of the things which he possesseth.

Luke 9:24 (KJV) For whosoever will save his life shall lose it: but whosoever will lose his life for my sake, the same shall save it.

On the other hand, there are some of us who think that as children of God, we are entitled to His blessings to make us wealthy. After all, God owns the cattle on a thousand hills, and His promises to bless us financially seem to be littered in the scriptures. Here are some of them:

Malachi 3:10 (KJV) Bring ye all the tithes into the storehouse, that there may be meat in mine house, and prove me now herewith, saith the Lord of hosts, if I will not open you the windows of heaven, **and pour you out a blessing, that there shall not be room enough to receive it.**

Proverbs 21:20 (KJV) **There is treasure to be desired and oil in the dwelling of the wise;** *but a foolish man spendeth it up.*

Luke 6:38 (KJV) **Give, and it shall be given unto you; good measure, pressed down, and shaken together, and running over, shall men give into your bosom.** *For with the same measure that ye mete withal it shall be measured to you again.*

Proverbs 10:22 (KJV) **The blessing of the Lord, it maketh rich,** *and he addeth no sorrow with it.*

Over the years, I have been confused by these apparent contradictions. In my youth, I resolved the impasse in my mind by allowing myself to be influenced by the loudest, most credible voices, credible in terms of the fame or stature of the messenger. This was easy since most people preached about prosperity, particularly when I was a fledgling Christian in the 1990s. The prosperity gospel was preached by just about every big-named preacher. "Name it…Claim it", they said. Christians were expected to be blessed beyond measure. They claimed that this was part of the more abundant life that Jesus promised in John 10:10.

The problem was that this prosperity gospel failed to acknowledge the plethora of scriptures that oppose their central theme regarding money. They just turned a complete blind eye to them and instead insisted that anyone who failed to be blessed must have unconfessed sin in our lives somewhere, or we just didn't have enough faith. This "gospel" was about money, but that was just part of it; it was also about faith and power. Either way, failure to achieve the blessings that they promised for doing the things that they demanded was blamed on us and not where it should have been—an error in their doctrine.

I recall an experience as a babe in Christ, totally influenced by this faith doctrine when I prayed privately and fervently that God would turn water into juice for me. I wanted to see His power at work. I was really committed to God. I just needed faith to make it happen. So, I kept that water in my refrigerator for weeks waiting on the change. I fasted. I prayed. Every day, I looked at that glass with an abundance of hope, but nothing happened. It didn't change. Eventually, I thought that the problem was that I was looking with my eyes rather than with faith. So, I decided to drink some of it, knowing that it would turn into juice in my mouth. After all, isn't this how the water turned to wine in Jesus' first miracle? Well, my water didn't change! Honestly, I am really embarrassed to even think about my foolish behaviour then. But I was trying what they preached. I was having the kind of faith that could move mountains. Or so I thought. But what I was doing was learning, growing, and developing. I learned then that a miracle isn't something to stuff my ego with. Miracles have purpose, and the purpose is never egotistical or to satisfy selfish pleasures. Today, as I previously discussed, I have come to realize that what I was doing was testing God in a manner that Jesus taught us not to.

Haply, right around the time that I started to mature in Christ, the prosperity gospel started to wane. Full disclosure, I never believed that the gospel should be used as a tool to become rich. In fact, I was disgusted by this concept. When more and more preachers spoke out against the prosperity gospel, I was quite pleased to see it die a slow, yet steady, death. Unfortunately, prosperity was eventually followed by the seedtime and harvest gospel. At least that's what I called it. People were told that if they wanted to be blessed, they must give to their church. More specifically, a lot of them were told they must give to their pastor. They framed it as the ointment that fell down Aaron's beard, then went down to the skirts and garments. I heard multiple persons use Psalm 133:2 to support themselves. So, this time, we had to take care of our pastor, who, once blessed, would be the catalyst of our financial blessings. No blessings for the pastor, no blessings for the congregation! I had a major problem with this. I fully support pastors, and I support paying them as well as the church can afford. Jesus made it clear that the labourer is worthy of his hire. However, what some persons were doing was something quite nefarious.

While our prosperous pastors enjoyed the good life in big cities at the expense of their members, most of whom were poorer than they, evangelists in remote, impoverished countries all over the world suffered, hardly being able to convince the same pastor to support their ministry. This was hypocrisy, I thought, and manipulation and intimidation, at its worse. Fulltime and devoted Evangelists could suffer, but our pastors had to be taken care of with material abundance. What's worse, the poor bought into this because they were hoping that these religious leaders could, through God, turn their financial malaise into abundance. The persons who bought into this more were the persons who could less afford to. This was my biggest problem. For example, I watched with despair and disdain when Pastor A visited Pastor B's church and preached to Pastor B's congregation that they must be grateful for having such a great pastor. They were admonished to show their gratitude by paying off Pastor B's mortgage, buying him an expensive car and, making sure Pastor B became debt-free. As you probably can guess, the favour was returned when Pastor B visited Pastor A's church a few weeks later and made the same demands of Pastor A's members. A religious scam is how I labeled this.

Time after time, I have observed the transformation of the prosperity gospel. Today, it looks like success. It's been dressed up in a fine suit, called by a different name, but its underlying principles are the same. Christians are to be successful at whatever we do. As people of God, we must excel; we must be the top and not the bottom; be a lender and not a borrower; be the head and not the tail. But none of these attributes are God-like. None promote humility; none are about helping the poor; none project God's image; all are about the self. It has become clear to me that one of our enemy's (the Devil) consistent strategies against the Church has been to keep Christians focused on ourselves and our worldly treasures. The enemy's response to Jesus' statement that we cannot serve God and mammon seems to be to try to make the two inseparable in our minds. This is what Paul meant when he told Timothy that there are some persons who believe that gain is godliness.

*1 Timothy 6:5 (KJV) Perverse disputings of men of corrupt minds, and destitute of the truth, **supposing that gain is godliness**: from such withdraw thyself.*

The Bible has many warnings for the rich, including warnings that came directly from Jesus Himself (see scriptures below). It is illogical that there could be so many scriptures warning us about something so specific, meanwhile other scriptures directing us to pursue the same thing so fervently.

Luke 6:24 (KJV) But woe unto you that are rich! for ye have received your consolation.

1 Timothy 6:17 (KJV) Charge them that are rich in this world, that they be not highminded, nor trust in uncertain riches, but in the living God, who giveth us richly all things to enjoy;

Proverbs 11:28 (KJV) He that trusteth in his riches shall fall; but the righteous shall flourish as a branch.

James 1:9-11 (KJV) ⁹Let the brother of low degree rejoice in that he is exalted: ¹⁰But the rich, in that he is made low: because as the flower of the grass he shall pass away. ¹¹For the sun is no sooner risen with a burning heat, but it withereth the grass, and the flower thereof falleth, and the grace of the fashion of it perisheth: so also shall the rich man fade away in his ways.

Luke 18:24 (KJV) And when Jesus saw that he was very sorrowful, he said, How hardly shall they that have riches enter into the kingdom of God!

The reality is that when Jesus spoke about rewards and blessings, He was generally referring to Heaven. That's the same place where He admonished us to lay our treasures. We covered that extensively in the last chapter. Why would He ask us to not to lay treasures on earth, but simultaneously promote a life filled with earthly treasures? He wouldn't. He didn't.

The fact is that we will not all be rich. However, as we asserted in the last chapter, we will not all be poor either. God has a plan for the rich, which is why He blesses some persons with wealth. In that respect, riches are a special gift from God. Not all of us will have this gift, no more than all of us will have the gift of singing, or preaching, or helps, or administration, or any other gift. As with all other gifts, the gift of being blessed with riches carries a great responsibility.

Before we explore God's plan for the rich, let's define rich. When we use this term, generally, we are referring to those persons who have more than their daily bread. In other words, they are able to pay for all of life's necessities and still have more for their personal enjoyment.

Give

The Bible teaches us that we are our brother's keeper in more ways than just protecting them. We are admonished to be their keepers financially too. There are many scriptures about helping others, such as when Jesus taught us that we ought to GIVE to everyone who asks, not asking for or expecting anything in return. We have already seen how the underlying economic message of both Jesus and Moses was about helping the poor. In short, it was about giving. The new testament authors shared the same principle. Paul said in Ephesians 4:28 (KJV)

> *Let him that stole steal no more: but rather let him labour, working with his hands the thing which is good, **that he may have to give to him that needeth**.*

The concept of giving is based on God's image and Him expecting us to live according to that image. He has given so much to us. There is no way that we can repay Him for His goodness and loving-kindness. However, He has designed a way for us, not to repay Him, but to say thank you to Him for His benevolence to us. His design is that we give to others. We must pass it on. **There is an absolute responsibility for those who have money, time, and talents to help those that are in need**. Meanwhile, we are not to expect a reward (to be repaid—Misthos) when we give because giving is rewarded (gift—Apodidomi) in Heaven.

The Gift of Giving

Everyone will not have the same level of financial success, and some will have none. Jesus said that we would always have the poor with us (Mark 14:7). Moses also acknowledged that there would always be poor people within the children of Israel (Deuteronomy 15:11). The promises to bless Israel were intended for the nation (macroeconomy); not everyone would benefit equally. Because of that, both Moses and Jesus made provisions for the poor to be taken care of by those that had.

> *Deuteronomy 15:11 (KJV) For the poor shall never cease out of the land: therefore I command thee, saying, **Thou shalt open thine hand wide unto thy brother, to thy poor, and to thy needy, in thy land**.*

> *Luke 6:35 (KJV) But love ye your enemies, and **do good, and lend, hoping for nothing again; and your reward shall be great**, and ye shall be the children of the Highest: for he is kind unto the unthankful and to the evil.*

What is the reason why some people are blessed financially more than others? Is it because they know and have followed the "7-step" program that guarantees success where the rest of us do not? Of course, I'm using sarcasm concerning the 7-step program. I have heard about a lot of religious success programs, and I am always disappointed in them because they suggest intuitively that everyone can have the same results. This is impossible, and I assume that everyone who teaches this is aware of this fact. We all have different talents, abilities and gifts. In Romans, Paul said this about the gifts of the spirit:

> *Romans 12:6-8 (KJV) ⁶**Having then gifts differing according to the grace that is given to us**, whether prophecy, let us prophesy according to the proportion of faith; ⁷Or ministry, let us wait on our ministering: or he that teacheth, on teaching; ⁸Or he that exhorteth, on exhortation: **he that giveth, let him do it with simplicity**; he that ruleth, with diligence; he that sheweth mercy, with cheerfulness.*

Did you see it? The gift of giving? God gives riches to whom He desires. All of these qualities that Paul listed are spiritual gifts, and he includes giving as one of them. Giving is a spiritual gift because those of us who can give were blessed by God to have something to give, just like every other spiritual gift starts with God. In addition to that, notice here that Paul also articulated the same message that we drove home earlier, that when we give, we are not to have any strings attached to it. The Common English Bible version puts verse 8 this way:

> *If your gift is encouragement, devote yourself to encouraging. **The one giving should do it with no strings attached.** The leader should lead with passion. The one showing mercy should be cheerful.*

We must give without expecting a reward. The gift of giving is confirmed in 1 Chronicles 29.

> *1 Chronicles 29:11-12 (KJV) ¹¹Thine, O Lord is the greatness, and the power, and the glory, and the victory, and the majesty: for all that is in the heaven and in the earth is thine; thine is the kingdom, O Lord, and thou art exalted as head above all. ¹²**Both riches and honour come of thee**, and thou reignest over all; and in thine hand is power and might; **and in thine hand it is to make great, and to give strength unto all.***

There are some very interesting things about this scripture.

- First, doesn't it almost mirror portions of the Lord's prayer? "Thine is the kingdom, and the power and the glory" (Matthew 6: 13). God is exalted and we are to recognize Him as the Exalted One. It is His Kingdom, not ours, and as such, we are to honour His judgements and decisions about everything associated therewith, including those whom He will bless with the gift of giving.

- Second, verse 12 says that riches and honour come from God. Anyone who attains wealth only gets it by the gift of God, both Believers and non-Believers. The Bible confirms this in Psalm 75:6-7, that promotion comes from God.

- Third, God gives this gift to whom He chooses. See the latter part of verse 12 of 1 Chronicles 29 and verse 7 of Psalm 75. The Living Bible (TLB) version interprets the Chronicle scripture this way "and it is at your discretion that men are made great and given strength."

In our pursuit of greatness or wealth, we ought to recognize where it comes from…God. Many persons set out to obtain success by getting degrees, work experience, developing their talents, and taking risks (for example, starting a business). Many of us actually achieve success when we do these things. Many Christians have this same testimony about how they got their education, worked hard, and took advantage of opportunities when they arose. Such blessed persons have no challenge acknowledging God as the ultimate source of their success. However, our recognition of God as our success is often very short-sighted. We tend to think that God blessed us because He loves us and wants to give us good things for us to enjoy this life. While some of this is true, there is some selfishness built into it, and we know that selfishness does not reflect the image of God. The part that we minimize is that God blesses us to help others.

If we chose to allow this selfish outlook to permeate our lives, there will always be a reason to limit our almsgiving. When our income supports it, we will want bigger homes, fancier cars, more luxurious vacations, better investments, higher quality stuff. It never ends.

Do you have the gift?

How do we identify if we have the gift of giving? I'd say it's about as easy to identify (or difficult, depending on your vantage point) as any other spiritual gift. Someone with the gift of singing just has to sing, and the gift would be easily heard. A gifted preacher needs only preach and see how people's hearts are challenged toward God. The gift of wisdom is revealed by listening when a wise person speaks on issues. Likewise, the gift of giving is seen in all who are blessed financially. We have already seen that riches are a gift from God. **The reason you were blessed with a lot of money is that the gift of giving has been bestowed on you!** That's why it's so easy for many rich people, whether Christian or not, to give back when they come into their wealth. But one does not have to be wealthy to have this gift, just have more than enough for yourself; have more than your DAILY BREAD. That's the true mark of this gift–having abundance.

The rich ruler in Mark 10 was gifted by God, but he did not appreciate that, as 1 Chronicles 29:11 says, the gift is God's. The glory is also God's. This means that we ought to glorify God with all of His gifts to us, not just gifts like preaching, prophecy, etc. We are also to glorify God with the gift of giving. The ruler, not understanding this, left Jesus sad because he was very wealthy. And because he chose not to glorify God with his gift, Jesus declared that it's difficult for him to enter into the Kingdom of God.

I can already hear the choruses of mean people quoting that they don't have a gift of giving and trying to use this as an excuse not to give to others. That is a mischaracterization because we have extensively covered how God wants us to be in His image and that His image means being inward-out focused. We have to care for others as much as we care for ourselves. We can't do this if we are selfish and mean-spirited. Consequently, while some persons have a special gift for giving, we are all expected to participate in giving, even if we only have 2 cents (mites) like the widow in Luke, or our last meal like the widow of Zarephath.

The Problem with Money

Before money was invented, mankind traded goods and services. The process is known as barter. In order to obtain goods or services that they needed, person A had to find another party, person B, who had the items or expertise that they desired, and they had to negotiate with person B to obtain the items they wanted. As you can imagine, the challenge was that they had to find someone who simultaneously wanted the goods or services that Person A possessed. This was further complicated by the fact that they had to determine the values of each item. Also, both had to have sufficient quantities to sell to the other person in exchange for what they bought, to ensure a fair trade occurred. The process must have been very difficult.

Money was invented to solve this problem. The solution was to create an item that could be exchanged by the purchasing party in lieu of their goods or services. Instead of Person A having to find someone who wanted their goods or services, they only needed to exchange the items they got from Person B with something that Person B could use to purchase anything else they wanted from anyone else. However, to do this, the item would have to have certain characteristics. Some of the key characteristics are that it would have to:

1. Be accepted by a lot of people

2. Be something that is easy to exchange between parties

3. Enable the value of different items to be compared to each other

4. Store its value so that when needed by the receiving party, they can reliably estimate its worth for another trade

While money solved the key problems of barter, it created many problems of its own. Here are some of the problems that I have found in money:

1. Because it has the ability to store value, it encourages greed

2. It promotes an arbitrary value on labour

3. It promotes scarcity. Persons are discouraged from providing goods or services that are undervalued

4. It promotes crimes and wars. Some people who lack marketable skills seek illegal means to obtain goods and services that they desire

5. It promotes misfocus on worldly wealth at the expense of righteousness

6. It discourages giving. People are too often inclined to give smaller denominations (e.g. $1 or $5)

Money may not be the root of all evil, but it certainly has contributed a fair share to it.

Unrighteous Mammon

Luke 16:9-13 (KJV) ⁹And I say unto you, Make to yourselves friends of the mammon of unrighteousness; that, when ye fail, they may receive you into everlasting habitations. ¹⁰ He that is faithful in that which is least is faithful also in much: and he that is unjust in the least is unjust also in much. ¹¹If therefore ye have not been faithful in the unrighteous mammon, who will commit to your trust the true riches? ¹²And if ye have not been faithful in that which is another man's, who shall give you that which is your own? [13] *No servant can serve two masters: for either he will hate the one, and love the other; or else he will hold to the one, and despise the other. Ye cannot serve God and mammon.*

To me, this is one of the most confusing things that Jesus taught because it seems to suggest, at first glance, He is instructing us to pursue wealth. However, nothing could be farther from the truth. No, Jesus was teaching us the same message as in the Sermon on the Mount.

In these verses, Jesus reminds us of some subtle yet important truths about money. He teaches that we are stewards of God's money. In verse 12, He refers to "another man's" things. The other man is God. Therefore, there are two parties to this parable; the manager, who represents you and me on the one hand as stewards, and God, on the other hand, as the Owner/Lord. Only when we allow this fact to permeate our hearts, can we really understand how to be faithful with money. Our money does not belong to us. It belongs to God. Is God glorified when we selfishly hoard money for ourselves? No!

In the parable, the manager was mismanaging his lord's assets. We, too, are guilty of mismanaging when we use money contrary to God's will. Instead, we must use money wisely **and faithfully**. If we are faithful with the least (i.e., money), we will be faithful with much (i.e., untold riches in Heaven). Conversely, if we are unfaithful with our money, we will also be unfaithful with heavenly blessings. Moreover, He says that if we are faithful with another man's assets (God's), we will likewise be faithful with our own, and vice versa. Jesus is reminding us that our money does not belong to us and that He wants us to use it for His purpose. He made the same point in the parable of the talents in Matthew 25.

Wealth

Another key lesson that Jesus taught is that wealth on this earth cannot compare to the wealth we will have in Heaven. In Luke 16:10, He calls money "least," but He calls heavenly riches "much," drawing a clear distinction between the two. Then in verse 11, He specifically calls this world's wealth "unrighteous mammon" while referring to heavenly wealth as "true riches." Dear Lord, please help us to see the true riches of Heaven. **Having wealth, in itself, may not be sinful nor wrong, but placing wealth above God is.** It is also sinful to hoard wealth while others suffer around us.

Jesus said, "That which is highly esteemed among men is an abomination in the sight of God" (Luke 16:15). The esteemed thing that He is referring to is the value that men placed on money. God does not have the same outlook on money as we do; after all, money is only a commodity. While we might value "things," God does not.

Later in Luke 16, Jesus told a parable about a rich man and Lazarus. He explained that Lazarus was a beggar. He had sores all over his body. He didn't have much to eat. Meanwhile, the rich man had everything he wanted. He had nice clothes and ate the best food. He had the kind of life that most of us dream about. But he refused to help Lazarus. After they both died, their fortunes were reversed. It was in Hell that the rich man realized that the selfish pursuit of riches was antithetical to God's image and expectations for us.

Jesus gave us a litmus test for our faith in wealth. Are we prepared, if asked by God, to sell everything and give the proceeds to the poor (not that anyone is asking you to)? Jesus said that it's difficult, but not impossible. This leaves a modicum of hope for the wealthy. But attached to that hope are His sharp cutting words "a rich man shall hardly enter into the kingdom of heaven." For our rich friends, Jesus clarified this. He was speaking about persons who trust in riches as opposed to persons who have riches. The implication of this is that it's hard for a person who places riches above God to inherit the Kingdom of Heaven.

When I was a Vice President in a retail bank in The Bahamas, I often had to make unpopular choices when my executive colleagues wanted to be unfair in their dealings. Many times, I had to break rank and oppose decisions that were unfair. Many times, I faced termination for standing up for right. I did this because I trusted in God even if it meant losing my high paying job. God blessed me with the job. The job provided me with some wealth. I worked a lot of long hours to keep the job. However, the job was only a tool. It was not the prize. Ultimately, the prize is being with Jesus. When the two conflicts, we must serve God, not mammon.

PERSONAL APPLICATION
GIFT OR LOAN?

Jesus teaches us to give, but most of us have supplanted the word give with the concept of lending. When you give something away, there is no thought or consideration for getting anything back in return. That's a gift. When you lend, at a minimum, you expect to receive the principal (amount loaned) back, or its financial equivalent. In other words, when you lend, you want to get your money back or receive something worth the same amount as what you loaned out. If you're a bank, you also expect to receive interest and some fees along with that (i.e. profit).

Jesus said, give, and it shall be given unto us, pressed down and shaken together men will give into our bosoms (Luke 6:38). Many people understand this to mean that we are to expect to receive blessings when we give. When we look at the distinction noted above between giving and lending, isn't it closer to lending when we expect to get something back in return? If I give expecting something back then I'm not truly giving, am I?

Part of the problem with Believers is that many of us may not fully grasp the concept of giving. We are taught that if we want to be blessed, we must give, but by definition, giving suggests the absence of an expectation of a return. What then must we do? We give and leave the rest to God. He blesses whom He will. When we give, not expecting a reward, we are behaving like God, who has given so much to us with no expectation of repayment. Frankly, we can never repay God for His goodness to us. Furthermore, because He has given so much throughout our lives, anything we give today is only a fraction of His manifold blessings from our past. We can never repay Him for all He has done for us considering that Jesus, who made the whole earth that we enjoy, decided to give His life violently to save us.

Since we can never repay God when it comes to giving to us, it would automatically disqualify us from expecting further blessings from God when we give to others. We receive far more than we give. Furthermore, whatever we decide to give would have first been given to us by God, whether it be by Him giving us health, strength and ability to work, or by Him blessing us with a source of income.

There is another anecdote when it comes to giving that I find rather interesting. It relates to the concept that what I am giving (or lending) is not my own asset. Instead, they are assets that God has entrusted in me. Therefore, if I give expecting something back in return, I am truly lending. Using this definition of lending, if I lend something that is not mine, this means I am leveraging. In a financial sense, leveraging is the use of debt to acquire assets and it is very risky in business. Debt is what happens when I borrow someone else's assets (usually cash) to use for my benefit.

As Christians, we believe that we do not own the assets that we have possession of, but that God owns them (the earth is the Lord's and the fullness thereof). When we give expecting something in return, we are in essence trying to gain personal benefits by using assets that we do not own. We are leveraging God's assets for our personal benefit. Rather than investing for our personal profit, God expects us to invest for His benefit. This was the underlying message of the parable of the ten talents. The servants were given the master's money. Only those who invested and yielded a return for the master was invited to "enter into the joy of thy lord" (Matthew 25:21 and 23). The servant who did not invest was cast away (verse 30). Likewise, if we decide that God's assets are solely for us to benefit from, rather than for God, we too will be cast out.

A final thought. If it were true that we are to receive blessings when we give, what happens after that? Do we keep it for ourselves, or do we continue to give? When people get excited about Luke 6:38, I often get confused as to why they are so excited about getting such financial blessings when all they will do is give it away anyhow. This is because my expectation would be that the person who gives as a response to God's goodness and mercy to them, will continue to give because their underlying reason actually expands–i.e. God's goodness to them just increased as a result of the blessing. This means they should want to give even more.

I would also expect that anyone who gives expecting to amass wealth as a result of our giving, is getting the whole message corrupted because this sounds like we only intend to use God to get wealth, then we forsake God's tenet of giving once we have abundance. Of course, God would see straight through us and as Jesus would say, "they have their reward," meaning that they are not impressing God with their behaviour.

Jesus confirmed this concept in Luke 14 when he said:

Luke 14:12-14 (KJV) [12] Then said he also to him that bade him, When thou makest a dinner or a supper, call not thy friends, nor thy brethren, neither thy kinsmen, nor thy rich neighbours; lest they also bid thee again, and a recompence be made thee. [13] But when thou makest a feast, call the poor, the maimed, the lame, the blind: [14] And thou shalt be blessed; for they cannot recompense thee: for thou shalt be recompensed at the resurrection of the just.

Giving, therefore, for Christians is not about a reward in this life. It is about laying up treasures in the life to come.

Chapter 9

Kingdom Hope
(Good News for the Poor)

Good News for the Poor

The disciples of John the Baptist, while he was in prison, told John about Jesus and the mighty miracles that He was doing. When John heard this, it caused him to wonder if Jesus was the Messiah. John asked his disciples to go directly to Jesus to find out from the horse's mouth. The story is found in Luke 7 below:

*Luke 7:18-22 (KJV) [18] And the disciples of John shewed him of all these things. [19]And John calling unto him two of his disciples sent them to Jesus, saying, Art thou he that should come? or look we for another? [20]When the men were come unto him, they said, John Baptist hath sent us unto thee, saying, Art thou he that should come? or look we for another? [21]And in that same hour he cured many of their infirmities and plagues, and of evil spirits; and unto many that were blind he gave sight. [22]Then Jesus answering said unto them, Go your way, and tell John what things ye have seen and heard; how that the blind see, the lame walk, the lepers are cleansed, the deaf hear, the dead are raised, **to the poor the gospel is preached**.*

Jesus knew that once John heard this, he would understand that Jesus was, in fact, the fulfilment of the prophesy found in Isaiah

*Isaiah 61:1-3 (NLT) The Spirit of the Sovereign Lord is upon me, **for the Lord has anointed me to bring good news to the poor**. He has sent me to comfort the brokenhearted and to proclaim that captives will be released and prisoners will be freed. [2]He has sent me to tell those who mourn that the time of the Lord's favor has come, and with it, the day of God's anger against their enemies. [3]To all who mourn in Israel, he will give a crown of beauty for ashes, a joyous blessing instead of mourning, festive praise instead of despair. In their righteousness, they will be like great oaks that the Lord has planted for his own glory.*

One day, when Jesus went into a synagogue, He was given the scroll of the book of Isaiah. He used that opportunity to tell everyone that He was the fulfilment of this prophesy. The text is found in Luke 4:15-19.

While these are excellent Bible verses to know, what I found most profound is the meaning behind the prophesy. The NLT version summarizes it by the words "Good News for the Oppressed." What is the good news? They are listed in the prophesy directly as follows:

a) Bring good news to the poor

b) Comfort the broken hearted

c) Free the captives

d) Let everyone who is mourning know that the time of the Lord's favour is near. They will be given

    i. A crown of beauty

    ii. Joyous blessings

    iii. Festive praise

The prophesy then speaks about their righteousness, alluding that all of the above will be available to the righteous. Jesus' summary of the good news, however, is more specific. Here's what He said about it:

a) The blind see

b) The lame walk

c) Lepers are cleansed

d) The deaf hear

e) The dead is raised

f) The good news is preached to the poor

It is most interesting that in each example above, other than one, Jesus listed an ailment then indicated that the good news was that the ailment was cured. The blind were cured by receiving their sight; lepers were cleansed from their leprosy; the deaf were able to hear; the dead were raised to life. However, in the case of the poor, He did not say that they were made rich or given financial blessings. It seems that despite

His absolute commandments that we help the poor, Jesus did not come to earth to make the poor rich. Instead, He came to give us good news; the good news is that if we live righteously, we have hope. The hope attached to the good news is found in verse 2 of Isaiah 61

> *He has sent me to tell those who mourn that **the time of the Lord's favor has come, and with it, the day of God's anger against their enemies.***

The time of the Lord's favour has come. This is the foundation of Jesus' message to the Jews that they ought to repent, for the kingdom of God is at hand. That's the same good news that Jesus always tried to motivate His disciples with–that their reward is coming. Notice that the scripture links something else to the Lord's favour; the day of God's anger against their enemies. This means that the favour will happen concurrently with the day of judgement, when God will judge us according to our work.

The good news for the poor is about Heaven! It is not about money; it is not about eradicating poverty; it is not about wealth redistribution; it is the hope that the poor will have eternal blessings, provided they live righteously.

Work-the burden of the Poor

> *Mark 14:7 (KJV)* ***For ye have the poor with you always,*** *and whensoever ye will ye may do them good: but me ye have not always.*

We shared in the last chapter that the role and responsibility of the rich is to share. They are admonished to lay treasures in Heaven. One way to lay treasure in Heaven is to give to the poor. We also clarified that the rich are people who have been able to lay treasures on earth. The ability to lay treasures on earth means that one has been blessed with more than one's daily bread; more than enough to cover one's necessities. Although giving may be one of the primary responsibilities of the rich, and although Jesus pronounced blessings on the poor, that they will inherit the kingdom of Heaven, these are not meant to insinuate that the poor is excused from responsibilities. On the contrary, there are many scriptures which show the burden of the poor.

We previously noted in Ephesians 4:28 that Paul said that we must not steal, but rather that we ought to work. Here is the same scripture repeated from the New Living Translation version:

Ephesians 4:28 (NLT) If you are a thief, quit stealing. **Instead, use your hands for good hard work**, *and then give generously to others in need.*

An even stronger scripture on the responsibility of the poor is found below:

2 Thessalonians 3:10 (KJV) For even when we were with you, this we commanded you, that **if any would not work, neither should he eat**.

The poor must work to take care of themselves. Able-bodied persons have a duty to get out there and work. The book of Proverbs has a number of scriptures about work. Here are a few:

Proverbs 13:4 (KJV) The soul of the sluggard desireth, and hath nothing: **but the soul of the diligent shall be made fat.**

Proverbs 12:24 (NLT) **Work hard and become a leader; be lazy and become a slave.**

Proverbs 14:23 (NLT) **Work brings profit**, *but mere talk leads to poverty!*

Proverbs 6:10-11 (NLT) [10]A little extra sleep, a little more slumber, a little folding of the hands to rest– [11]then poverty will pounce on you like a bandit; scarcity will attack you like an armed robber.

All of these scriptures combine to suggest that the definition of the poor does not include persons who are capable of work, but refuses. It is meant to refer to persons who are incapable of work. Jesus definitely does not support lying and dishonesty. This is how I would define a person who purports to be poor, but in fact simply chooses to take advantage of the rich.

Poor Man's Religion

Hebrews 11:24-26 (NLT) [24]It was by faith that Moses, when he grew up, refused to be called the son of Pharaoh's daughter. [25] He chose to share the oppression of God's people instead of enjoying the fleeting pleasures of sin. [26] He thought it was better to suffer for the sake of Christ than to own the treasures of Egypt, for he was looking ahead to his great reward.

What a remarkable scripture. It aligns perfectly with everything that was presented above and in earlier chapters. Once Moses grew up, physically and spiritually, he made an amazing choice when it came to wealth. He chose to forego his wealth in Egypt in place for suffering with God's people. He chose poverty over riches. He gave up all of his wealth to serve God. However, the suffering was not his ultimate objective. His goal was something that verse 26 describes as "his great reward." Like Moses, we too should be looking for our great reward…Heaven.

Jesus said that it is difficult for people with riches to inherit the Kingdom of Heaven.

> *Matthew 19:24-30 (NLT) ²⁴I'll say it again–it is easier for a camel to go through the eye of a needle than for a rich person to enter the Kingdom of God!" ²⁵The disciples were astounded. "Then who in the world can be saved?" they asked. ²⁶Jesus looked at them intently and said, "Humanly speaking, it is impossible. But with God everything is possible." ²⁷Then Peter said to him, "We've given up everything to follow you. What will we get?" ²⁸Jesus replied, "I assure you that when the world is made new and the Son of Man sits upon his glorious throne, you who have been my followers will also sit on twelve thrones, judging the twelve tribes of Israel. ²⁹And everyone who has given up houses or brothers or sisters or father or mother or children or property, for my sake, will receive a hundred times as much in return and will inherit eternal life. ³⁰But many who are the greatest now will be least important then, and those who seem least important now will be the greatest then.*

Peter's response is quite interesting. He wanted to know what his reward would be for forsaking everything and following Jesus. So much for those who thought Peter, as a businessman, was wealthy. He left everything, including his business, and now seem to be hoping, or even jockeying, for a position in Jesus' kingdom. Don't forget that the Jews were looking for a king to assume the throne of David. They were looking for Israel's elevation in the world. Having been with Him for a while, they understood that Jesus was truly the promised Messiah, the King of the Jews. So, Peter wanted to know what he was going to get for his loyalty to the future King.

Jesus assured him that they would have prominent roles in His Kingdom. He told them that they would sit on twelve thrones as judges over the twelve tribes of Israel. But that promise is deferred for when Jesus sits on His throne, which does not happen until judgment day. That's when they are to receive their reward. Jesus then encouraged them to remain humble and to accept a low role in the world today, because "many who are the greatest now will be least important then, and those who seem least important now will be the greatest then."

While Jesus may have said that it will be difficult for the rich to inherit the kingdom, He also said that it is not impossible. Part of the reason is the time and effort it takes to become and maintain riches. I have had a lot of experience pursuing worldly prosperity. I was moderately successful at it. Read more about my story below.

PERSONAL APPLICATION

In this personal application, I have truly gone personal. I have written a little about my personal history and experience with moderate success in hopes that it can help someone else going through some of the things I faced.

At the age of 18, I moved out of my parent's home and went straight to work as a Bahamian Customs Officer. I was the top graduate among 50 recruits. During my tenure there, I took a leave of absence to obtain a bachelor's degree in Accounting. I stayed in Customs for about 9.5 years and left when I graduated from university.

First, I attended The College of The Bahamas, a 2-year college, where I graduated as valedictorian. After COB, I attended Acadia University in Canada. I took and passed the CPA exams, which is an American accounting designation, in one sitting during my final year at Acadia.

I was one of the highest recruited accounting graduates for the accounting firms. In just over 3 years, I was promoted to Audit Manager. A short while later, I left the auditing firm and took a managerial position in the offshore banking industry. I stayed in the offshore industry for a few years then went into the retail banking industry. Within a few years (relatively speaking), I became the Chief Financial Officer of one bank then moved to another as Chief Internal Auditor, then Chief Credit Risk Officer. Today, I am the founder and president of Money Managers Co. Ltd., a Bahamian financial services company.

I had a moderately successful career. Prior to leaving the banking industry, I was out there working hard and being promoted. However, my life was turned upside down. The things I held dearest to me became secondary. My spiritual life suffered tremendously because the job was consuming all of my energy. The deception of having God and mammon took its toll on me. Even though I thought my career was a sign of God's blessings, I shamefully forsook my relationship with Him for my professional development. I became focused on the gift and not the Giver. I spent more time reading text books and articles to develop myself than I did reading the Bible. I spent more personal time doing work than I did in prayer. Once success started to come, it became a monster that needed to be fed. I had to keep up with the industry changes. I had to work harder than anyone else because I felt that this was part of the call of God for my life. I felt called to succeed. Meanwhile, God was in the back seat until, at some point, I unwittingly realized what was happening to me. That's when I recognized that I needed things to change. I was too devoted to the job. I was too devoted to success. Success eventually created a void that more success could not fill.

That was when I knew I was not living life more abundantly. That was when I realized the deception of success. That's when I yielded my life back to God, forsaking the riches of success. I felt like Moses who left the riches of Egypt in pursue of a better promise. My life has never been better than it is now that I have refocused it on God.

This story is not meant to suggest that none of us should pursue success, however, it is meant to advise Believers not to be fooled into pursuing success at the expense of your relationship with God. We must seek God's kingdom first. This acknowledgement was the beginning of God's revelation to me about His Kingdom, and the foundation of This Book.

Patrick James McFall

Chapter 10

Kingdom Microeconomics (Personal Budget)

Money is vital to the quality of our lives. We need money to buy food, shelter, safety, clothing, and other necessities. Jesus acknowledged this fact in the Kingdom Sermon on the Mount (see Matthew 6:32). But as Christians, money is essential for another reason. One of the key biblical truths and a foundation of Kingdom economics is to GIVE. Needless to say, we cannot give if we don't have anything to give. Conversely, **for many people with noble intentions, the extent of our giving is constrained by our ability to manage our personal finances.** This is debilitating many Christians who seriously want to be good stewards. In other words, sometimes our financial deficiency and inability to give to the Lord is the result of us wasting money. The more money we waste, the less money we have to give to God. In this sense, **knowing how to manage our money is an integral, albeit less talked about part of our Kingdom lives.**

Knowledge is key

Everyone knows that there is a cost for education, and the cost has been a barrier that has prevented some persons from obtaining advanced degrees. Conversely, **there is an economic cost for financial illiteracy (or ignorance).** I'm talking about real money here. I would venture to say that the cost of ignorance exceeds the cost of education because educated people, on average, earn more money over their lives, which yields a positive return on the cost of the education. I will never forget a former colleague of mine who foolishly told me that the best I could hope for in pursuing a university degree was to break even. He argued that while he understood that I would earn more money after I graduated, he said, at best, it would only be sufficient to recover the amount of money that I would lose from the years I would not be earning a salary while in university, coupled with the high school fees that I would have to pay. Sadly, he had no clue what he was talking about. Disregarding his advice was the best thing for me. I went on to finish university, passed the CPA exams, and within a few years, my income exceeded my pre-university salary by more than 300 percent.

Ignorance costs us every day in different ways and varying degrees. It costs us because we have to settle for lower-paying jobs when we are not qualified for better positions. It costs us when we get stuck in certain positions because we didn't advance ourselves, or when we don't get the raise in salary that we asked for. It costs us when economies decline and we get terminated, or when economies change and we don't qualify ourselves to take advantage of the opportunities that become available due to the change.

Just as there is a financial cost for ignorance, there is similarly an economic cost for being financially ill-prepared, whether the reason is for poor planning, incomplete planning, or no planning at all. Inaction, or delayed action, has the same impact as being unprepared, even when you have the best plan possible. I have certainly had my share of experiences with this. Once, when I learned about a reasonably priced multi-family vacant land in a great community, I lost the sale because I pondered about it too long. Someone else moved in faster and bought it while I reflected. I was thinking while someone else was acting. **Planning is good, but delaying a good plan is bad.**

On the other hand, I have been able to take advantage of more than my share of opportunities because I studied, prepared myself, made a plan, and executed the plan timely. It's this experience that has helped this son of a taxi driver and a sales clerk, who worked as a low-level government employee for almost ten years, adjust the trajectory of his life to become a certified accountant, a chief financial officer at a bank with over a billion dollars in assets, and become totally debt-free at the age of forty. I am a witness that **it is not too late to make sensible changes that will positively alter the trajectory of your life.** God is able to accelerate opportunities for late bloomers like I was.

Financial literacy is much more comprehensive than these few examples. The OECD (Organisation for Economic Co-operation and Development), in its attempt to aid member countries in enhancing financial literacy, grouped financial behaviours into two categories, namely financial control and financial resiliency. Financial control deals with behaviours such as budgeting, responsibility for financial decisions, making considered purchases, punctual payment of obligations, and monitoring financial affairs. Behaviours indicative of financial resilience include saving, ability to face external shocks, long-term goal setting, and making informed choices of financial products (The Central Bank of The Bahamas, 2018). We will attempt to cover some of these subjects.

Financial Planning 101

This chapter is designed to help persons who may be struggling with managing their finances due in part to financial illiteracy. It's a basic review of budgets and financial planning from my personal perspective. It is intended to help persons who have little to no knowledge about these subjects. **However, as much as God's people are destroyed because of our lack of it, knowledge is NOT the entire solution to our financial malaise. As James preached in his epistle, faith without works is dead. We must also ACT if we are to achieve financial stability.** If we fail to act, we are no better off having knowledge.

Definitions: The definitions below are intended to assist with understanding some of the financial terms used in this section.

- Assets - An item that you own which has value and is able to be liquidated into cash or can be otherwise used to generate cash.

- Own - An asset over which you have legal right to use, sell, or dispose and the benefit of using and/or the proceeds of selling will accrue to your benefit.

- Owe - An unpaid liability.

- Liability - A legal obligation to pay or repay a third party, mostly due to a previous transaction for which you received some benefit.

- Net worth - The monetary value (dollars and cents) of your total assets minus your total liabilities.

- Budget - An estimate of your income and expenses for a given period.

Have a Plan

Lack of financial planning may cause you to fail to obtain some of the things you want in life. It can cause you to make bad decisions, which can negatively affect you and your dependents. If you have a good job that's paying you well, you may assume that you're making enough money to meet all of your needs. However, without proper planning, hidden or unexpected costs can cause you to suffer needlessly because you did not prepare properly for different events in your life. While we cannot prepare for every eventuality, there are some that are <u>inevitable</u> (such as retirement), or <u>predictable</u> (such as a downturn in the economy), or <u>possible</u> (such as accidents, bad health, or even death). We have to prepare for all of these, and a great part of the preparation is financial. **We must have a financial plan for all of life's possibilities.**

The list of bad decisions that can result from not having a financial plan is endless. You may, for example, continue working a low paying job because you don't understand how it's impacting your ability to improve your financial stability. You may be spending more money on unnecessary things than you realize, all because you don't have a plan. You may be wasting money on pleasures for today at the sacrifice of a better life for tomorrow, or at the sacrifice of helping others. Or, you might not be considering opportunities to pursue a better education because you may believe it's too costly and thereby forego the potential benefits resulting from better education. A formal financial plan is very important, and I encourage everyone to have one.

Most of us have informal financial plans, which, although not great, is still better than none at all. One of the biggest challenges for most people is that they lack the discipline to stick to their financial plans. Part of the reason is that their plans are often informal, and therefore the specifics are difficult to remember, much less keep. Anyone who finds themselves unable to save at the level they desire, or are unable to grow their assets like they had hoped, or are unable to keep the focus on their financial priorities, must not rely on informal plans. They need formal, written plans.

Not having a formal financial plan to guide you is very risky. It can cause you to lose focus on the important things in favour of things that are timely or convenient. In other words, it can cause you to waste money on unimportant things. For example, instead of saving for retirement, many persons in their twenties assume they will have more time for this and opt to spend excessive monies on things that make them feel good (e.g., fashion, food, entertainment, etc.).

Not having a formal plan may also cause you to be unprepared for good opportunities or important life events. For example, purchasing a home involves more than a desire. It requires planning and savings. Without a plan, you will not know how much savings is needed for the quality of home that you desire, and if a good opportunity comes in a great neighbourhood, you may lose out and have to settle for something less than desired because of the lack of planning.

A formal plan is especially recommended for the following persons:

1. Persons with low income

2. Persons who have lost their jobs

3. Persons with significant financial responsibilities (e.g. parents),

4. Persons who are retired, or near retirement

5. Persons who want to make material purchases (e.g. buy a home or other big-ticket item, attend university, make investments)

6. Persons who lack financial discipline

7. Persons who want to improve their savings

8. Anyone else who just wants to manage their finances better

If you fall into one of these categories, this chapter will help you. Please note, however, that the examples we provide in this book do not include any income tax consideration because there are no income taxes in The Bahamas. Persons who are subject to income tax should be sure to include its effect on their financial plan.

I would give my family an A-minus if I were to grade our financial planning history. We have been meticulous in developing our plans. We knew how much interest we would have to pay on loans and developed action plans to repay them all early, thereby saving tens of thousands of dollars in interest and fees. We managed our investments closely to ensure that we received all interest and dividends to which we were entitled. We set a date for becoming debt-free, as we did for every major financial goal that we had, and we achieved all of them, most of which were done within our schedule. We also kept our expenses in line with our plans. Even though we could afford more, we limited the treasures that we wanted to build on earth. We regularly discussed our plans, and we worked them together. Not only that, but we also followed God's economic plan and gave lots of money, time, and support to others who needed it, without expecting rewards. We left little to chance.

Step 1 – Prepare your Wish List

Each of us has a very good idea of the things that we want in this life. We all tend to desire similar basic assets: house, car, and investments. Most of us want to get married and have children. All of us want to have enough money to retire and live out our senior years comfortably. These assets and financial desires are sometimes called our "wish list." These are the things that we wish or desire to have in our lives.

Our wish list is usually very extensive and normally very costly. Let's assume a relatively normal 20-year-old who might have the following wish list items.

1. University degree

2. House

3. Car

4. Wedding and honeymoon

5. 2 children–educated up to university level

6. At least one vacation trip per year

7. Retirement at 65 with sufficient assets in a retirement fund

This is a simple example of some of the big-ticket items a person may wish to have over the course of their lives. It does not include day to day living costs such as food, clothing, and entertainment. When added together, the simple wish list will cost millions of dollars. Most of us don't have this much money or assets and will never amass them at any given time in our lives. However, over our total life span, assuming we live to retirement age at 65, most of us earn sufficient income to make our wish list items a reality. The biggest problem with not achieving our wish list is seldom due to the income we earn. It's mostly due to poor planning. Another problem is that more often than not, we wait too late to get serious about financial planning. These issues, together with the high cost of the wish list items along with the timing issue (that we don't have the cash now, but that we have to earn it over our lives), heighten the need for us to manage our finances to ensure that all our wish list items are achieved.

Frankly, the above wish list is too simplistic because there are hidden costs in these items that must be considered. For example, houses and cars experience wear and tear. No house will last 40 years, nor car last 10 years without regular repairs and maintenance. Both houses and cars need insurance, and these can also be very costly. Any long-term financial plan will also be affected by inflation. Things usually cost more over time, and the longer the time period, the more the impact inflation will have on the cost of the items. Inflation will impact each of these wish list items. Unforeseen emergencies can also impact financial plans materially. As we age, our health normally deteriorates, and this can be very costly. Many of us whose parents live long lives find ourselves having to care for our parents. This also can be very expensive. Things just happen!

Some persons may have lofty desires. Having dreams of grandeur may be an obstacle to effective planning. We must be careful not to raise our expectations beyond our reach. Our financial plans must, therefore, be realistic, and this involves including the hidden costs noted above. Otherwise, we are making plans that are intrinsically elusive. We have to be specific but also reasonable. We also have to be flexible.

My family decided that our primary economic wish list item would be financial independence. This would be the dominant consideration for all financial decisions that we made. It governed all other decisions. For example, when we decided we wanted a home, we looked at numerous residential building plans. Some of them were beautiful and fully representative of the job status that we held at the time. I was a corporate senior manager in an offshore firm, making a very comfortable salary. My wife was an office manager at a thriving orthodontic practise, also earning a good salary. We could afford almost any home that we desired, but we had to weigh that desire against our underlying objective of financial independence. We realized that as the cost went up, our ability to become independent went down. We, therefore, settled on something that we thought was a very nice home, but one that would not materially hinder our most important goal. We did the same for every major financial decision in our lives.

These highlight some of the challenges and the importance of personal financial planning and management. Now that we have set up the basics, let's begin to develop a financial plan.

Setting a wish list requires you to identify the cost of each item, the time frame needed to accumulate the funds, and the priority of the item, as shown in the example on the next page.

Goal	Cost	Time to Achieve	Priority
Retirement	Estimate the annual income needed during retirement and multiply it by 25	65 – Current Age	
Home	Estimate the cost to build or purchase	Desired Date – Current Date	
Property	Estimate the cost to purchase	Desired Date – Current Date	
University	Estimate the annual cost of tuition, room/board, books, and cost of living and multiply it by the number of years to complete the degree	Desired Date – Current Date	
Car	Estimate the cost of the vehicle	Desired Date – Current Date	
Debt Free	Using the amortization schedules or estimates, determine the total debt expected on the desired date of payoff.	Desired Date – Current Date	

Once the wish list is prepared, you will need to know the following to manage how well you will achieve them:

1. How much you have today

2. How much you save each month/year

Step 2 – Prepare your Net Worth Statement

Every Believer should know what they own and what they owe. This is the foundation on which your financial plan is built. Financial experts call this your net worth. It's a simple assessment of all of the assets that you own and the liabilities that you owe to others. The net worth is normally recorded based on a specific date because it changes regularly. For example, every day, you pay bills from your 'cash on hand' (purse or pocket), from your credit card, or from your debit card. After every payment, your net worth changes because the amount of cash assets you own, or liability you owe, would have changed due to the payment. Therefore, determining your net worth requires you to, in essence, take a snapshot of your assets and liabilities at a specific point in time, usually at the end of a given month. Below is an example of a simple net worth statement.

Sample Statement of Net Worth
As at December 31, 20XX

ASSETS	Value	
Cash on hand	$	75.00
Cash in Bank	$	1,000.00
Total Cash	$	1,075.00
Car	$	5,000.00
Furniture	$	3,000.00
House	$	150,000.00
TOTAL ASSETS	**$**	**159,075.00**
LIABILITIES		
Credit Card	$	1,500.00
Car Note	$	2,500.00
Mortgage	$	125,000.00
TOTAL LIAILITIES	**$**	**129,000.00**
NET WORTH	**$**	**30,075.00**

Note: This is a very simplistic example and it is not representative of any actual person. Any similarities to a person are totally coincidental. This example assumes you have included all assets that you own even if you have not paid for it in full, and all bills that you owe even though you haven't paid for them yet. Accountants call this accrual-based accounting. It basically means that you have captured every asset and every liability in the statement.

There are other assets that you may own (e.g., pension plan assets, timeshare, investments, utility deposits, etc.) or liabilities you owe (e.g., alimony, medical bills, lease commitments, taxes, etc.) that are not included in this example. You will have to examine your own situation to determine your personal net worth.

Your net worth is determined by subtracting your total liabilities from your total assets. If the resulting figure is negative (i.e., your total assets is less than your total liabilities), this means that you have a negative net worth. If, as we noted, the statement is based on accrual accounting (i.e., it includes all monies due to you and all liabilities that you have to pay), this is bad! It means that you are financially underwater. You may have borrowed money, but there are insufficient assets to show for it. It's also possible that your assets have depreciated or been used up faster than you paid for it. Whatever the reason, this is not a good position to be in because it means that you have bills that you are responsible for paying, but you don't have enough assets to pay them from.

On the other hand, if your net worth is positive, this means that you have sufficient assets to pay for the liabilities you owe, and if you were to use your assets to pay all of your bills, you will have residual assets remaining. This is good!

However, just knowing your net worth is not sufficient. You also need to know what is happening with them over time. You need to know if it is growing or if it is contracting. For example, if you have a negative net worth of $5,000 (your liabilities are $5,000 more than your assets), as we have noted, this is bad. However, if three months previously, your net worth was a negative $100,000, this paints a much better picture. This tells me that you have accumulated $95,000 in net assets in three months. Said another way, your growth in total assets over the last three months has exceeded your growth in total liabilities over the same period by $95,000. You are improving, and this improvement is good.

Therefore, it's important to calculate your net worth regularly for you to see how things are progressing over time. This ability to see your progress allows you to make adjustments when things are not advancing as expected. For example, you may have made a wish list to save an additional $10,000 within two years in order to make a down payment on a parcel of land. To ensure that you achieve this, you decide to review your net assets quarterly (every three months). As a result, you have targeted quarterly expected growth of $1,250, which is $10,000 divided by eight quarters (which is two years). To confirm your progress, you should prepare your net worth statement every three months to see how you are progressing. If at any of these quarterly reviews, your savings have not increased by $1,250, this puts you in jeopardy of reaching your $10,000 target in 2 years. Consequently, you will know how you need to adjust your monthly savings going forward to get back on track and ensure you meet your goal.

Step 3 – Prepare your budget

A budget is a statement that comprises two main sections–income and expenses. You will have to list all sources of income (places you earn money) in the income section with an estimate of the amount that you expect to earn over the set period (usually a month). In the expense section, you will have to list all of your expected expenditures over the same period. Below is a simple sample of a budget statement. Once again, this is not based on any actual person. Any resemblance is purely coincidental.

Sample Budget
For the Month of December 20XX

	Amount	EXPENSES		
INCOME		Tithes/Offering	$	307.00
Salary	$ 3,000.00	Mortgage/Rent payment	$	750.00
Overtime/Tips	$ -	Property taxes	$	-
Bonus	$ -	Homeowners Association Fees	$	-
Investment income	$ 50.00	Car Note Payment	$	250.00
Interest income	$ 20.00	Car maintenance/gas	$	200.00
Other	$ -	Bus/Taxi/Other Transportaton	$	-
TOTAL INCOME	**$ 3,070.00**	Electricity	$	300.00
		Phone	$	75.00
		Other utilities	$	200.00
		Food	$	500.00
		Bank charges	$	30.00
		Health & other insurance	$	200.00
		Entertainment	$	200.00
		Other expenses	$	200.00
		TOTAL EXPENSES	**$**	**3,212.00**

SUMMARY	
Income	$ 3,070.00
Expenses	$ (3,212.00)
NET INCOME	**$ (142.00)**

As with the net worth statement, this is only a simple example, and it excludes income tax considerations. You will have to prepare a budget based on your specific circumstances. The key is to remember to include all sources of income and all expenditures that you expect over the exact same period.

One of the difficulties in budgeting is estimating expenses. It cannot be done effectively without having a strong commitment to knowing where all your money goes. To help you with this, you will have to be disciplined to account for every payment that you make, no matter how small, over a period of at least one month. There are apps available for download at very low costs (some free, but may require a small payment if you choose to use more of the services they offer). If you can't use an app, you can just use a ledger (or piece of paper).

Once you figure out where you will record them, you need to jot down every payment that you make. Try to keep every receipt to match each payment. Once this has been done, you will have to summarize the expenses into categories similar to the categories that are included in the example. Feel free to add new categories that make sense to you. Once they are categorized, you then have the tool to make budgets going forward.

Once the budget has been prepared, you then have to evaluate what it means. If the net income is expected to be negative (like our example), this alerts you that you have to make some changes. Negative net income means that your income is insufficient to cover your expenses. The continuous shortfall in income will first affect your cash balances, as you will have to deplete your cash to make up for the deficit. In other words, because the income that you earn is not sufficient to pay for your expenses, you have to get the shortfall from another source, which normally is your savings. The impact of this is that your net worth will be reduced, which is not the desired effect. Prolonged persistence in this state will eventually result in a reduction in other assets or in borrowing money to make up the difference. This kind of behaviour signals a major red alert. Wise planning anticipates this problem and makes adjustments before things get too bad. You should immediately make adjustments somewhere. The basic options are to supplement your income, reduce your expenses, or borrow money to make up the shortfall. This is where wisdom and self-discipline come into play. We caution you to borrow wisely, for example, only if the funds will be used for important transactions that will bring you long-term benefits greater than the value of the amount borrowed.

Potential adjustments to supplement income include the following. Please do not make any changes without fully understanding the ramifications of that decision, as it is possible that the specifics of your situation may not lend to any of these options being viable for you. It is important to research each option fully before pursuing them.

1. Take a second job (e.g. part time)
2. Find a better paying job or position in the same company
3. Enhance your portfolio of income generating assets to increase earnings. For example:
    a. If you own investments, you may wish to change strategy to an income generating strategy
    b. You may wish to move any excess cash held in a bank account to an investment account
    c. If you own a house, you may consider renting it.
    d. You may also consider selling your single-family home and purchase or construct a multiple family dwelling to earn rental income
    e. You may also consider selling your car and invest the proceeds. Use public transportation instead.

On the other hand, you may have to make changes on the expense side. To evaluate this area, first you need to separate the expenses into mandatory and non-mandatory expenses. Mandatory expenses include mortgage, rent, car payments, utilities, insurance, food, and some entertainment. As Christians, we are also expected to pay tithes and offering. These should be included in your mandatory expenses.

Next, look at voluntary expenses and decide which ones you can shave to get you to a positive budget. Keep cutting voluntary costs until your budget is positive. However, keep in mind that some otherwise mandatory expenses are actually voluntary to a certain degree. For example, rent is normally considered mandatory, but a portion (or maybe all) of it may be voluntary if you can find alternative living arrangements such as moving to a less expensive location, moving back with parents, shared living experiences with a relative or close friend, etc. Likewise, expenses like utilities could be voluntary if we consider things like the usage of air conditioners or switching to energy-saving bulbs.

Balancing a budget with limited resources can require a lot of intelligence, effort and creativity on your part. It may also require the assistance of a professional financial planner. You should seek help if you become overwhelmed with the challenge.

See below adjusted budget reflecting hypothetical changes:

Sample Budget - ADJUSTED
For the Month of December 20XX

INCOME	Amount	EXPENSES		
		SAVING	$	100.00
Salary	$3,500.00	Tithes/Offering	$	457.00
Overtime/Tips	$ -	Mortgage/Rent payment	$	750.00
Bonus	$ -	Property taxes	$	-
Investment income	$ 50.00	Homeowners Association Fees	$	-
Interest income	$ 20.00	Car Note Payment	$	250.00
Other	$ -	Car maintenance/gas	$	250.00
TOTAL INCOME	$3,570.00	Bus/Taxi/Other Transportaton	$	-
		Electricity	$	300.00
		Phone	$	75.00
		Other utilities	$	200.00
		Food	$	450.00
		Bank charges	$	30.00
		Health & other insurance	$	200.00
		Entertainment	$	100.00
		Other expenses	$	100.00
		TOTAL EXPENSES	$ 3,262.00	

SUMMARY

Income	$ 3,570.00
Expenses	$(3,262.00)
NET INCOME	$ 308.00

The shaded items in the adjusted budget above reflect the changes to the original budget. Salary is adjusted to reflect our hypothetical person taking on a part-time job. Car fuel has increased to reflect the need to transport to the other job. Food, entertainment, and other expenses were evaluated and determined that these can be cut and still fit into the individual's lifestyle.

One of the important residual effects, and intended results, of budgeting, is saving. In the discussion above, we have not considered savings as a mandatory expense. Most financial planners, including this author, believe that it is important to budget for savings as part of your expenses and that savings should be considered as a mandatory expenditure in your budget (see savings added to the adjusted budget above). The amount projected for savings may be changed depending on your future financial needs, but once established, savings should be set aside before other expenses are made. Consider Joseph in the Bible for a perfect example of the importance of savings.

Step 4 – Assess and Adjust

Once you have determined your wish list and prepared your net worth statement and budget, you have to assess your ability to meet the wish list using the information available. Use your net worth statement to identify your starting position–i.e., your net worth (in the example is $30,075). Of this amount, the liquid assets total $1,075. Use your budget to determine your monthly savings. This is your net income (in the adjusted budget example, it is $308 per month). Be sure to include your savings expenditure line in the budget if you have budgeted for savings as an expense (in the adjusted budget example, it is $100). The total of these is $408 (i.e. $308 + $100).

To determine if you will have sufficient cash to make a big-ticket purchase, you will have to start with the amount and date you wish to make the purchase. Let's assume the targets are five years and $30,000. Based on your cash on hand today and your savings per your budget, you will be able to save approximately $25,555 by the end of 5 years. This is calculated as follows:

Cash today	$1,075	Per Net worth Statement
Savings Year 1	$4,896	$408 multiplied by 12
Savings Year 2	$4,896	$408 multiplied by 12
Savings Year 3	$4,896	$408 multiplied by 12
Savings Year 4	$4,896	$408 multiplied by 12
Savings Year 5	$4,896	$408 multiplied by 12
TOTAL	$25,555	

Once again, this is a very simplified example because it does not factor in changes during the five years (e.g. prices might increase–which is inflation, you may lose a job, you may experience an unforeseen emergency, you may get a promotion, or annual cost of living increases, etc.). It also does not consider interest income. This projection should be made with a lot of conservatism and scepticism, understanding the risk of error in projecting anything into the future. In this simplified example, you will not have sufficient cash to meet the targets of $30,000 in year 5. Because of this, you will need a plan to address the shortfall. Possible options include:

- Deferring the purchase. If you extend the date you hoped to make the future purchase, you may be able to use the additional time to accumulate the extra savings needed to make the purchase.

- Cut the cost of the purchase. Some big-ticket purchases can be adjusted downward in terms of cost without losing the full benefit of the purchase. Examples include buying a smaller home, attending a less expensive university, having a smaller wedding, buying a cheaper car, purchasing less costly furniture, etc.

- Selling other assets to finance the purchase. Other assets might include a car, vacant land, time share, etc. which can be sold to make up the shortfall. However, these options usually have a time delay factor because they often take time to be liquidated (i.e. sold). This time factor should be considered along with this option.

- Borrowing. In some cases, borrowing is a viable option as long as it is managed effectively. We discuss the use of debt in more detail below.

- Cancelling the purchase. This is extreme, but in some cases it may be necessary. For example, although you may wish to purchase a time share property, your finances may not support it because of other pressing priorities. Rather than insisting and causing untold damages to your life and health, you may consider just not buying it at all.

Using the above information as a guide, you should be able to manage the financial affairs of a basic and simple family. Anything more complex is beyond the scope of This Book.

Treasures

At the beginning of this chapter, we shared how managing our finances has important spiritual implications. In the preceding section, we discussed the importance of reviewing our expenditures and making adjustments we deem necessary. Let's turn our attention to the spiritual nature of personal financial management.

Jesus commanded us not to lay up treasures on earth, but instead to lay them up in Heaven. He also said that we cannot serve God and mammon. Remember also that as Christians, we are commanded to give. What does all of this have to do with managing finances? Easy. One of the ways we determine where our treasures are being laid is by looking at our budget and statement of net worth. Where are we spending money? In the Kingdom Sermon on the Mount, Jesus said prophetically "where your treasure is, there will your heart be also" (Matthew 6:21 - KJV). Are you spending more on entertainment than in your church's offering? What is the ratio of your monthly savings to your monthly almsgiving? These kinds of questions can be quite revealing of who we are. Attempting to answer such questions can be very enlightening and may highlight the need to make adjustments in order to be obedient to God.

Malachi 3:8 (KJV) asks, "Will a man rob God? Yet ye have robbed me. But ye say, Wherein have we robbed thee? In tithes and offerings." It's easy to understand how to rob God of tithes. We do it when we fail to give 10% to Him. However, it's not so easy understanding why the prophet said we rob God in our offering. I submit that when our offering is a small fraction of our entertainment, we may be robing God. Likewise, when our monthly offering is infinitesimal to our personal savings, then we are laying treasures on earth at the expense of treasures in Heaven. The challenge with these measures is that the amount of offering that we should give is not defined in the Bible. There is no right amount nor wrong amount of offering to give. It's entirely a personal decision, and God wanted it to be this way. Because of this, I have no guidance to share with you on what is reasonable. God wants us to decide for ourselves because He wants to know what is in our hearts; or put the way Jesus said it, He wants to know where our heart is.

Other important financial stuff

Other important things that Believers must consider as early as possible include insurance and retirement planning. On these matters, we refer the reader to their insurance and retirement planning experts for advice. However, readers should be aware of the significant risk involved in not being adequately prepared in the event of loss of life, accidents, etc. The impact is not only to yourself, but to your dependants and loved ones. We strongly advise you to consider coverage in these areas.

PERSONAL APPLICATION
DEBT MANAGEMENT

To the extent you may benefit from it, I offer a little about my personal experience with debt management and how we used it to purchase assets while simultaneously pursuing a debt free life. Over our lives, my wife Lavette and I have borrowed money when we needed to make purchases but didn't have sufficient cash at the time. However, we limited these situations to large assets such as cars, a home, and certain investment opportunities (time share and employee stock options at materially discounted prices). In each case, we ensured that there were no early repayment penalties because our strategy was always to repay each loan early, thereby reducing our overall financing burden.

First was the 7-year car loan which we paid off in about 3 years. Then there was the 10-year time share note which we paid off in about 2 years. The home came next, but before that was repaid, we purchased investment properties and stocks in the company where I worked using debt because we didn't have sufficient cash assets at that time. We decided to use debt because we expected that the value that we would receive from the assets would outweigh the cost of financing. We anticipated this because we ran the numbers. I am a qualified accountant so I was trained for this part, but if you are not, please seek help from a professional. We were right and the returns justified the decision to get into debt.

Systematically, we paid the highest interest rate loans off first, then we went on to the other loans. Within 10 years, all were paid off and we have been DEBT FREE ever since. It's now been more than 12 years. In fact, our planning has enabled us to start a micro lending company to assist other people who need a little help meeting important expenses, similar to how we needed help in our lives.

In addition to repaying debt early when possible, I suggest that the key things to consider when it comes to managing debt are:

1. Look out for high origination fees. Before you commit, ask around to see what the fees are. If one lender is willing to offer you financing, it's likely other competitors will also. Money is homogeneous but the loan fees are not, and neither is the quality of service. Search for the best price, factoring in quality of service such as convenience (access to your loan balances on demand, remote access through Apps and online, ability to apply remotely, etc.).

2. Other loan fees can be astronomical. The same concept as #1 applies to other loan fees. Fees include early repayment fees, late fees, insurance. I have seen customers who were told that if they repaid the loans early, they would have to pay out the full term of the facility. This means that they would have had to repay all future interest and fees as if the loan proceeded according to the payment schedule. They were unaware of this. It's important to know the facts about your loan. Ask!

3. Compare the interest rates. Interest rates will vary slightly between institutions. Don't be afraid to ask the institution for their range of interest rates.

4. Credit Card interest and fees. Be very mindful that credit card is a special loan product–it's a revolving credit. This means that once your credit limit is approved, you can charge and make purchases up to that limit. If you repay the balance, your approved limit remains available for future purchases without having to go back to get a new limit approved. These card products attract very high interest rates (most exceeding 20%, and higher if it's a cash transaction). Credit card fees are usually also very high and include fees for over-limit, cash advance, additional card requests, late fees, among others. Find out what each card company's fees are and make smart decisions. Note: Most cards have a grace period whereby they will not charge you interest if the entire balance is paid off in full by the grace period date. Take advantage of this where you can.

5. Be mindful of the loan term. Some institutions will try to attract you by offering lower monthly payments. You should know that your payment can be lowered by the lender offering a longer term to repay the loan. This option comes with a hefty price as the total interest that is paid by the borrower is normally much higher for longer term loans.

6. Don't be deceived with debt consolidation offers. For the same reason as #5, debt consolidation usually results in lower monthly payments, but the interest that you will have to pay on the back end is usually significantly higher. Use debt consolidation wisely, sparingly or not at all.

Patrick James McFall

Section 4

Chapter 11

Conclusion and Summary

Ecclesiastes 12:13-14 profoundly summarises everything that The Preacher wrote in the book of Ecclesiastes. The scripture says (KJV):

¹³Let us hear the conclusion of the whole matter: Fear God, and keep his commandments: for this is the whole duty of man. ¹⁴For God shall bring every work into judgment, with every secret thing, whether it be good, or whether it be evil.

I can find no better words than these to summarize everything that is written in **Thy Kingdom Come**. In it, we discussed the Commandments of Jesus, and the resounding message is that in order to be counted as a child of God, and in order to live in the image of God, we must know them and follow them, with the aid of the Holy Spirit.

Jesus bought our salvation and gave us grace through His life, death, and resurrection. This brought us to the precipice, the door if you please, of the Kingdom of Heaven, but this Kingdom is not yet. First, Jesus will separate those of us whom He will invite into the Kingdom from those who will be refused entry. In Matthew 25:32-34, Jesus referred to this process as dividing the sheep from the goats. This process is the same that The Preacher referred to when he wrote about God bringing "every work into judgment."

What is the point of this judgment if not to dole out rewards? Jesus confirmed this assertion in Revelation 22:12 (KJV), where He said:

*And, behold, I come quickly; **and my reward is with me**, to give every man according as his work shall be.*

We have coherently revealed that Jesus did not advocate nor support the concept of sowing financial seed as a means of receiving financial blessings from God. However, Jesus often spoke about rewards. In the above scripture, which is part of His last quoted message in the Bible, and in which He discusses the end of this world as we know it, Jesus still had our rewards on His mind. This speaks to the importance of these rewards to Him, but it reveals a lot of other things about these rewards. If His rewards were earthly financial rewards as many assume, then He would have no occasion to still be talking about rewards. Yet He did. This is because the rewards that Jesus constantly talked about are the rewards that we will receive when He comes back for us.

Very near to his death, Paul had an introspective look at his life. I believe he contemplated the many things he suffered. He was stoned. He was jailed. He was beaten with rods and stipes. He was robbed. He was fussed at. He suffered hunger and was often cold. Paul, not being the picture of success and wealth, affirmed what Jesus taught, and which we attempted to say in This Book, about the proper priority of money and wealth when he wrote the following:

2 Timothy 4:6-8 (KJV) ⁶For I am now ready to be offered, and the time of my departure is at hand. ⁷I have fought a good fight, I have finished my course, I have kept the faith: ⁸**Henceforth there is laid up for me a crown of righteousness, which the Lord, the righteous judge, shall give me at that day: and not to me only, but unto all them also that love his appearing.**

The treasure that we ought to focus on is not of this world. Our hope, and the thing that we love and are earnestly anticipating, is not of this world. Our life, our course, our purpose, is to do the will of God for the remainder of our existence here on earth. Then one day, we will receive our just reward.

Revelation 22:14 continues, "Blessed are they **that do his commandments**, that they may have right to the tree of life, and may enter in through the gates into the city." Our job now, nay our delight, is to fear God and keep His commandments because this is our ultimate purpose as human beings. It's no coincidence that The Preacher made this same observation in Ecclesiastes 12:13.

Many of us Believers have sought or are still seeking our God-ordained purpose, and we have somehow concluded that the revelation of our purpose is some sort of higher calling to do something specific, more so, something great on this earth for God. Too few of us are so gifted that we can wrap our talents in a box, tie a bow on it and call it our purpose. For the countless (billions) rest of us normal humans with no special abilities, no golden voice, no compelling charisma, no discernible skill, no special aptitude, no physical prowess; we spend many hours, days and years tormented, wondering where our place is on this earth. We have fallen prey to the manmade concept that purpose represents a special calling to do something special and that every person on earth has such a purpose. Therefore, when we fail to find our special talent, we meander aimlessly throughout our lives, feeling unhappy and depressed that we have not found our purpose. **The Preacher gives us our purpose, and it is to fear God and keep His commandments.**

This Book helped us see that the Law was given by Moses, but grace and truth came by Jesus Christ. Moses gave the laws, and out of great respect, we call them commandments. Moses' laws were intended to establish Israel as a kingdom. Jesus gave His commandments, yet many of us cannot identify what they are. We call some of them beatitudes, and others, we simply don't know that they are commandments. Jesus came preaching about God's Kingdom, trying to establish His Kingdom principles on earth as it is in Heaven so that we can be restored to our intended place– God's image.

Paul even spoke about the image of God in 2 Corinthians 4:4, defining Jesus as such. If Jesus is the image of God, then for us to be in God's image as He made us, we must follow Jesus' example. He didn't accumulate wealth, for He had no place to lay His head. He humbled Himself, being the Son of God, creator of the earth, God Himself–yet He suffered and died at the hands of His creation because it was the will of God. Jesus kept God's commandments because He loved God. I can go on and on, but suffice it to say that He practised what He preached in the Kingdom Sermon on the Mount. Therefore, He commands us to also keep these words of His, if we are to be the image of God as Jesus is.

Jesus commands that we are to pursue peace, mercy, love, humility, righteousness, giving, forgiving, etc. He taught us to go after these things more than money, food, clothing, and shelter. Most of us have been taught these tenets from our youth, but adhering to them is about as hard as life itself because we are not engineered to behave like this. Hence the warning that Jesus gave that "few there be that find it" when talking about His Kingdom. I pray to God that He opens our eyes to see and our ears to hear the unspeakable beauty of His love and grace toward us.

The Preacher, in writing about the things he learned throughout his fabulous, wildly successful life, concluded that all is vanity and vexation of spirit. This is what he said about his great achievements in Ecclesiastes 2:4-8,11 (KJV):

> *⁴I made me great works; I builded me houses; I planted me vineyards: ⁵I made me gardens and orchards, and I planted trees in them of all kind of fruits: ⁶I made me pools of water, to water therewith the wood that bringeth forth trees: ⁷I got me servants and maidens, and had servants born in my house; also I had great possessions of great and small cattle above all that were in Jerusalem before me: ⁸I gathered me also silver and gold, and the peculiar treasure of kings and of the provinces: I gat me men singers and women singers, and the delights of the sons of men, as musical instruments, and that of all sorts.*

> **¹¹ Then I looked on all the works that my hands had wrought, and on the labour that I had laboured to do: and, behold, all was vanity and vexation of spirit, and there was no profit under the sun.**

Even in this unexpected place, I found the mysteries of the Kingdom. The Preacher called all of these worldly achievements, vanity. In **Thy Kingdom Come**, we talked about man's outward-in focused lives. We explained how this was selfish and ungodly because it does not produce the image of God in us. This, too, is what The Preacher found. That we spend all of our days seeking things that are full of vanity. This is because anytime we do things that promote ourselves excessively, we are selfish, and this is vanity, and it drives us away from God. The Preacher not only called these things vanity, but he also called them vexation of spirit. While he may have been referring to the spirit of man, these things are also vexation to the Spirit of God. We are admonished in the Bible not to grieve nor to quench the spirit. The pursuit of selfish goals is a vexation to the Holy Spirit.

The Holy Spirit is our Helper and our Guide to completing our purpose. But He is more. We cannot be adopted as children of God without the Holy Spirit coming into our lives. Once He comes, the good news is that He gives us gifts, including spiritual, physical, and financial gifts, that are intended to help us and our fellow Believers. If we use those gifts by giving back to and supporting others as well as ourselves, and follow the Holy Spirit, we will be found worthy of inheriting a place in the Kingdom of Heaven where we will live with Jesus and our Father forever. If not, there is no place in Heaven for us.

My prayer

Dear God and Father, thank you for being good and kind and merciful. You have sent Jesus who died for us, and He too is good and merciful and humble. He sent us the Holy Spirit, who is patient, and gentle, and good. You have shown us your nature, and we understand that because we are made in your image and likeness, we are expected to be like you. Please help us to overcome any element of selfishness and greed that may be hidden in our hearts. Forgive us as forgive others. May our eyes see, and our ears hear, and our minds comprehend the mysteries about your Kingdom. And may we, at the end, be found righteous, so that we may be found worthy to receive our reward when Jesus returns.

Amen.

Patrick James McFall

About the Author

Reverend Patrick James McFall is an accomplished minister, accountant and banker. He has had many academic and professional accomplishments including multiple executive management positions in the fields of finance (Chief Financial Officer), auditing (Chief Internal Auditor), and credit risk (Chief Credit Risk Officer) at large Bahamian banks. His academic achievements include the United States uniform CPA exams, Canadian Securities Course, many executive training courses, outstanding student award at Acadia University, and valedictorian of the College of The Bahamas.

Reverend McFall currently serves as an Associate Minister at Bethel Baptist Church, Nassau Bahamas, the oldest Baptist church in the Bahamas, and the longest continuing Baptist church in the Caribbean. Bethel Baptist was established in 1790. His ministerial experience includes youth Pastor at Golden Gates Assemblies of God, Nassau, Bahamas and multiple leadership positions throughout his life.

In addition to church, Reverend McFall has served other religious organizations, the most prestigious being the Progressive National Baptist Convention, USA, Inc., a US religious organization with over 2 million members worldwide. He currently holds the positions of budget chairman, board member and member of the Finance and Property Committee. He is also a director of one of PNBC's affiliated organizations and an approved lecturer of PNBC's Congress Classes.

He is the 5th of 6 children from the union of Reverend Pedro (deceased) and Yvonne McFall. He was born, and still resides in the city of Nassau, The Bahamas. Reverend McFall is married to Reverend Lavette McFall nee Bethel and they are proud guardians of A'Mya Maddison Elise Strachan.

Patrick McFall is available for book interviews and personal appearances. For more information contact:

Patrick McFall
C/O Advantage Books
P.O. Box 160847
Altamonte Springs, FL 32716
info@advbooks.com

To purchase additional copies of these books, visit our bookstore at:
www.advbookstore.com

*A*dvantage
BOOKS

Longwood, Florida, USA
"we bring dreams to life"™
www.advbookstore.com